Fig. 1: London and Westminster
Light Horse Volunteers pre-1801.

town. A bandmaster had to be found, instruments to be bought, and when all this was arranged the end result had to be presentable. Bands varied in musical ability from regiment to regiment; some were even considered to be a laughing stock, but the advent of a new commanding officer or bandmaster could soon alter this. At the other end of the scale a few bands attained a very high standard indeed; later several were to become amongst the foremost in the country. A few regiments decided not to compete and never raised a band. Amongst the others competition was keen; if the Hussars in the next county for example had a well mounted, well dressed and musically skilful band then there was every reason to make sure that one's own band should surpass it, in the same way that the skills of soldiering were always a matter for competition between regiments.

Most Yeomanry bands were at their best during the Victorian years, *i.e.*, from about the 1830s to 1900. After this date and the South African war, difficulties increased and very few regiments were able to maintain their mounted bands. During the Edwardian years therefore they eventually dropped out one by one and by 1914 hardly any remained, and were never to be re-raised. Instruments were kept for band concerts and so on; so too were the precious drum banners. One uses the word advisedly as several dated back to William IV and others from early Victorian days; often, as previously stated, the painstaking work resulting in beautiful examples of stitchcraft and embroidery at its best by the ladies of the regiment

The Drum Banners
Whilst the presentation of a Standard or Guidon was an event of importance in the life of a Yeomanry regiment, invariably reported in the county press and the regimental history (if any), acquiring a drum banner was apparently of secondary importance and seldom recorded. Nowadays paintings, prints and photographs are also quite rare. So for those with an interest in the subject today, the Sheet published in 1916 by Gale & Polden and now republished with this booklet is not only a valuable guide, but could also be decorative for the study wall. Our object therefore is to bring together as much surviving pictorial material and data as is possible. The centre of the Sheet illustrates the Standards and Guidons of the post-Boer War period, but this subject is outside our present scope, although it is hoped to devote a further publication to it.

The story behind the 1916 publication is interesting. Frederick Stansell of Bath, whose profession was a designer of wallpaper, was also a gifted artist and painted military pictures as a remunerative sideline. He was not always as accurate in detail as his colleagues Harry Payne and Richard Simkin with whom he was constantly in touch, and collaborated with them on occasion. The Army Museums Ogilby Trust has in its files interesting correspondence between Stansell and Harry Payne and two letters in particular throw light upon the production of the Gale & Polden Sheet. Drum banners of the Cavalry and Yeomanry were obviously a subject that interested him as far back as 1906 when a letter to Harry Payne dated 29 December 1906 relates how he had information about drum horses and banners of several Yeomanry regiments. In the same letter he tells Payne about a fellow enthusiast he had met at some earlier date: 'Benson Freeman is a Navy man but an authority upon the Yeomanry strange to say. A thoroughly good fellow. I went down to Portsmouth to lunch with him and the officers on the *King Alfred*. He is now on the China Station; I am sorry as it takes such a time in getting a reply to one's letters and my figures have to fit his mss. Of course after getting the details and making all roughs I pass them on to our friend R.S.

(Richard Simkin) to make the finished drawings for illustrations. I don't seem to have the time for that.'

It took a further 10 years before a firm order for the work was received from Gale & Polden[5] as a letter dated 9 February 1916 to Harry Payne tells. 'I got an order for 36 banners and Guidons (Yeomanry) from Gale & Polden and have taken advantage of a break of about a fortnight in the wallpapers to come down here and paint them. You know what an amount of notes etc. one wants to do a job of this kind. I don't know to what use they will put them. Some months ago I offered them a sheet of drum banners of the cavalry — regulars, being the only bit of heraldry left to the army, they would not take it up. They hesitated about the drum banner book and finally decided to postpone the publication, when suddenly they write for six banners of the regulars. These I did and they were very pleased with them and send now an order for 8 more regulars — 12 Yeomanry banners and 12 Guidons.'

In Edwardian days whilst postal and transport services were good, it would be difficult, if not quite impossible for a man in Stansell's position to travel the country inspecting the original items at various regimental headquarters. Local ones he could do but othewise he had to rely on any photographs he could obtain or by correspondence. It is thought that the latter was his main source and would probably account for any errors in the compositions he eventually presented for publication. One hopes therefore that the text submitted now will iron out some of these difficulties.

In the 1920s Stansell received a commission from John Player & Sons to provide paintings to be used for cigarette cards — one card given away in each packet of cigarettes . The order was for 50 cards to represent both the Cavalry and Yeomanry regiments and Royal Artillery drum banners. The series was published and issued in 1924 under the title 'Drum Banners and Cap Badges'. Numbers 24 to 49 inclusive dealt with the various Yeomanry regiments, on the back of each card a thumbnail history and, if converted into other arms, the new title of the regiment at that time. This gave Stansell the opportunity to revise some of his previous patterns. These cards are still obtainable from dealers at a reasonable price and therefore a cigarette card number from the series has been quoted for comparison with the Gale & Polden Sheet.

Post-War Drum Banners

In 1925, under the title 'Yeomanry Dragoon Battle Honour Scrolls', an A.C.I. ordered that: 'A complete set of Great War battle honour scrolls, ready for affixment, is to be issued to each Yeomanry Dragoon Regiment, including those regiments now converted into other arms, which were authorised to carry Guidons prior to reconstruction of the Territorial Army. -----'. Several regiments used the occasion to add similar battle honour scrolls to their existing drum banners or, as in one or two cases, acquired new banners where all principal battle honours could be displayed. This would have been an expensive item when one remembers that the

banners would be used for decorative purposes only, at band concerts, etc., when the kettle-drums on stands would have been on show.

The Gale & Polden Sheet

The Yeomanry drum banners were arranged as a frame surrounding the central portion illustrating the Standards. The arrangement of the banners is in the Order of Precedence as given in the Army List; however, it has been decided to arrange the present text in alphabetical order of regiments, as in the Army List, for ease of reference. A Chart (Fig. 1a) is shown with the titles as on Sheet but with an added number showing its place in the text, *i.e.*, Ayrshire — Chart No. 1 etc.

In the centre of this Chart are some random examples of the cigarette card series; the number of the particular card is given below it (Fig. 1a).

N.B.

(a) The title of the Army Museums Ogilby Trust is repeated several times throughout the text and is referred to as A.M.O.T. hereafter.

(b) Similarly there are several references to items in the Journal of the Society for Army Historical Research, referred to as J.A.H.R. hereafter.

(c) Many of the sources given are quite rare items and difficult to find nowadays but most are in the A.M.O.T.

Yeomanry Drum Banners from The Gale & Polden Sheet

The Ayrshire Yeomanry (Earl of Carrick's Own)

The story of this old Regiment is well documented in a fine Regimental History[1] where it is refreshing to find several references to the band. First mention is for 1845 when a Royal Standard was presented to the Regiment, the band taking up a position in the centre of a hollow square. There is no mention whether this band was mounted at that time, but by 1888 it was. Reference to this is made when the Bandmaster, Mr. R. J. Adams, who had held the position for 26 years, retired.

The difficulties of maintaining a band in a Yeomanry regiment at that date can be gathered from correspondence of 1897 when a Band Committee resolved to try and reduce expenses. It appears that the band was hired on a year-to-year basis and paid for by the officers. An advertisement for the post of Bandmaster brought three replies which make interesting reading. The first was from the serving German Bandmaster, Herr Iff. He wrote a blunt note from Glasgow on 27 March 1897.

To R.S.M. Burrell, A.Y.C.,
Dear Sir,
I have your letter of yesterday and in answer beg to say that as the officers of the Regiment find the expense of my band too high, I regret I cannot undertake to supply the music for the Yeomanry training. I remain, Dear Sir, Yours faithfully, Louis Iff.

A second letter from a Mr. Henry C. Sime of Ayr included a list of the instrumentation he would need for the mounted band:

---

5. Gale & Polden also published a Sheet of *Cavalry Standards, Guidons and Drum Banners*, a similar work by F. Stansell.

4 Cornets, 2 Horns, 1 Bombardou, 1 Euphonium, 1 Baritone, 3 Trombones, 1 Drum or Timpiana, equals 13. Reeds added at night 6, equals 19.

9 West Kent Yeomanry (Queen's Own)

10 Royal Glasgow Yeomanry (Queen's Own)

11 Lancashire Yeomanry (Hussar)

12 Duke of Lancaster's Own Yeomanry

13 City of London Yeomanry (Rough Riders)

14 1st County of London Yeomanry Middlesex (Hussar)

15 3rd County of London Yeomanry (Sharpshooters)

16 Lothian and Border Horse Yeomanry

8 Hampshire Yeomanry (Carabiniers)

7 Dorset Yeomanry (Queen's Own)

6 Royal North Devon Yeomanry (Hussar)

5 Royal 1st Devon Yeomanry

4 Derbyshire Yeomanry

3 Cheshire Yeomanry (Earl of Chester's)

2 Berks Yeomanry (Hungerford)

1 Ayrshire Yeomanry Earl of Carrick's Own

17 Montgomeryshire Yeomanry

18 Northumberland Yeomanry (Hussar)

19 Nottinghamshire Yeomanry (Sherwood Rangers)

20 Nottinghamshire Yeomanry (South Notts Hussars)

21 Oxfordshire Hussars (Queen's Own)

22 Shropshire Yeomanry

23 North Somerset Yeomanry

30 Yorkshire Dragoon Yeomanry (Queen's Own)

29 Yorkshire Yeomanry (Hussar) (Princess's of Wales Own)

28 Royal Wiltshire Yeomanry (Prince of Wales's Own Royal Regt.)

27 Westmorland and Cumberland Yeomanry

26 Suffolk Yeomanry (Duke of York's Own)

25 Staffordshire Yeomanry (Queen's Own Royal Regt.)

24 West Somerset Yeomanry

---

31 — PLAYER'S CIGARETTES. CAP BADGE. Yorkshire Dragoons Yeomanry. (Queen's Own).

40 — PLAYER'S CIGARETTES. CAP BADGE. 1st County of London Yeomanry. (Mxex. Duke of Cambridge's Hussars). Now and Cavalry Divisional Signals.

48 — PLAYER'S CIGARETTES. CAP BADGE. Lothians and Border Horse Yeomanry. Now 19th (Lothians & Border Horse) Armoured Car Coy., Tank Corps.

28 — PLAYER'S CIGARETTES. CAP BADGE. Shropshire Yeomanry. (Dragoons).

38 — PLAYER'S CIGARETTES. CAP BADGE. Dorset Yeomanry (Queen's Own). (Hussars). Now 94th (Somerset & Dorset Yeomanry) Brigade, R.F.A. (2 Batts.).

46 — PLAYER'S CIGARETTES. CAP BADGE. Oxfordshire Yeomanry. (Queen's Own Oxfordshire Hussars). Now 100th (Worcestershire & Oxfordshire Yeo.) Bde., R.F.A. (2 Batts.).

24 — PLAYER'S CIGARETTES. CAP BADGE. Royal Wiltshire Yeomanry, (Prince of Wales's Own Royal Regt.), Hussars).

37 — PLAYER'S CIGARETTES. CAP BADGE. Derbyshire Yeomanry. Now 24th (Derbyshire Yeomanry) Armoured Car Coy., Tank Corps.

44 — PLAYER'S CIGARETTES. CAP BADGE. West Kent Yeomanry, (Queen's Own). Now 97th (Kent Yeomanry) Brigade, R.F.A. (2 Battalions).

The third application was from a Mr. W. Eaglesham of Kilmarnock dated 23 March 1897, who stated:

Sgt.-Major Burrell, A.Y.C.
Dear Sir,
I shall be very pleased to supply band of 13 or 15 performers at the terms over, for the permanent duty of assembly to dismissal.
Yours truly, W. Eaglesham.

Followed by a detailed list of the instrumentation (and names of bandsmen) at a cost of £99; this was accepted. Mr. Eaglesham held the position until 1914.

As far as is known there is only one photograph of the mounted band before 1914, and that one of rather poor quality, but at least one can see that the kettle-drums are uncovered, that the bandsmen wear forage caps, and that the photograph must have been taken *c.* 1890-93, as infantry pattern helmets are still in wear by the rank and file.

It is not known when drum banners were obtained and there are no illustrations of them in use before 1914. Tho pattern shown on our sheet (Chart No. 6 and also on the 1924 Player's card (No. 29)) is a reasonably accurate representation: *i.e.,* on crimson cloth — a crown, a union wreath and scrolls top and bottom carrying the Regimental title, gold edging and fringe.

After World War 1 the band was re-formed in 1921. Following the award of Battle Honours from WW1, these, together with the 'South Africa. 1900-02' Honour already granted, were either added to the existing banners or placed upon new ones as shown on Fig. 2. They were arranged five on each side of the central design:

South Africa. 1900-02	Ypres. 1918
France and Flanders. 1918	Rumani
Gallipoli. 1915	Gaza
Egypt. 1916-17	Jerusalem
Palestine. 1917-18	Tell 'Asur

Fig. 2: Ayrshire Yeomanry, post 1924. Probably a new banner with W.W.1 honours.

Regimental history tells us that the band played at functions of all kinds and at the annual Races and Sport during the 1920s and 1930s when the drum banners would no doubt have been used for decorative purposes. A photograph of 1958 shows the dismounted band, 18 in number together with Bandmaster (W.O.1 Brace) and the Regimental Adjutant from the Royal Scots Greys, taken on the steps of Yeomanry House, Ayr, the drum banners as previously described arranged over the kettle-drums on stands.

[1] *The Proud Trooper.* By Major W. Steel Brownlie, M.C., T.D., M.A.; pub. Collins 1964.

The Berkshire Yeomanry

Whilst the earliest Troop of Yeomanry raised in the county of Berkshire was the Abingdon Troop, 1794-1828, the Hungerford Corps followed in 1831 and the title Hungerford was still retained in the Army List up to 1914 and later.

First traced mention of the band is in the *Reading Mercury* of 20 August 1842, reporting on a cricket match between Hungerford and an invitation side. 'The superior brass band belonging to the Hungerford Troop attended on the occasion and played some delightful airs'. This Corps obviously possessed a mounted band as the presentation of a fine pair of kettle-drums by the Major-Commandant, George Willes, was made in 1853. It can be noted that the title and crest include that of the Royal county of Berkshire, a title occasionally associated with the Regiment in later days but it does not appear in Army Lists or most other official documents.

4

In 1868 there is mention of the excellent band from Wantage, still going strong in 1880 as the band from D Troop, Wantage.

In an unusually disparaging article for the era the *Reading Mercury* stated concerning the annual inspection for 1876, 'The band was dismounted, and therefore presented a somewhat sorry appearance. Their performances too were neither of a melodious nor martial character'.

In his autobiography the well known artist R. Caton Woodville[1] tells how, as an officer in the Regiment in 1879, he marched the London contingent to Regimental HQ at Reading for the annual camp. He had some hard things to say about the band: 'Our band was a great laughing stock in those days, mounted on all kinds of horses, the drummer on a light grey shire horse. At camp some Troopers hid the drums in a pigsty and a couple of shaft buckets had taken their place', He also related how he, and presumably other young high-spirited officers: 'Saw a tar bucket and could not resist painting the drum horse with a regular pattern of round spots, such as depicted on Mr. Punch's horse. It had a good effect as the next year saw the re-formation of the band and an enormous improvement.'

This improvement is borne out from an extract in the *Reading Mercury* of 20 May 1882: 'The principal feature of this year is the band, which, through the liberality of the officers, has been entirely reconstituted and very much improved. An efficient Bandmaster has been appointed, and the band will now compare favourably, both for strength and efficiency with most of the Yeomanry bands in the kingdom. Nearly all the bandsmen are "double handed", and they play admirably every evening at the "Queen's", during the officers' mess.'

Photographs taken during the next 20 years or so show the band to be of smart appearance, whether mounted or dismounted. (Most of these pictures were taken at Abingdon, then in Berkshire but now of recent years in Oxfordshire.) In 1887 for instance, a photograph shows the entire Regiment mounted and in review order; the band on the right flank and nearest the cameras, readily identified by red and white helmet plumes, compared with the Regiment's all-white, and a drum horse in the immediate foreground. Other pictures taken at Abingdon around the turn of the century show an extremely smart mounted band, which, on first glance might be taken for Life Guards, the tunics having gauntlet cuffs and the collars laced in Household Cavalry style (Fig. 4). The drum banners are very fine although of simple design and much different from that shown on our chart. These banners, still in Regimental possession, are described as of faded rose colour, have silver edging with red line running through, and silver fringe, the interwoven letters R B Y C in silver with the Star and Crescent above (Fig 3). The pictures on Chart No. 13 and cigarette card No.39 are both totally inaccurate. Photographs of the dismounted band of

Fig. 4: Berkshire Yeomanry. Band outside the Town Hall, Abingdon (then in Berkshire) *c.* 1902.

Fig. 3: Berkshire Yeomanry. Date not known, believed 1880s.

1909, 1911 and 1912 do not show any drum cloths in use, and no other actual banner remains with the Regiment, so in the absence of any further evidence one has to query the authenticity of these illustrations.

The band was officially dismounted in 1912, struck off the strength in August 1914 and re-formed in post-war years.

My thanks to Mr. A. French, Assistant Curator of the 94th (Berkshire Yeomanry) Signal Squadron Museum, Windsor, for great assistance with these notes.

1. *Random Recollections*, by R. Caton Woodville, pub. London, Eveleigh Nash, 1914.

The Earl of Chester's Yeomanry Cavalry

The first mention of a band occurs in 1817, to be 13 in number, and provided with a uniform, whilst Colonel Sir John F. Leicester, Bt., purchased a portion of the instruments and employed a person to instruct the bandsmen. It is not recorded how long this early band was to function but the Regimental History[1] tells us that at a meeting held in Chester on 13 June 1848, the officers decided to form a band and a comprehensive set of rules was drawn up. A Mr. C. Wright was appointed Bandmaster and most of the instruments required were presented by serving officers, and also by former officers. These band instruments were to be engraved with the letters 'K C Y C' (King's Cheshire Yeomanry Cavalry) to mark them as regimental property, although these particular initials were soon to be out of date. On 26 January 1849 'Her Majesty signified her pleasure that the regiment should henceforth resume its first designation of the Earl of Chester's Regiment of Yeomanry Cavalry'.

In 1863 a new band of 15 members was formed and stationed at Macclesfield. It was probably about this time some attention was paid to the question of providing suitable drum banners, and several designs were submitted by Hawkes[2]. Whilst the designs for as many as six drum banners were at various times put forward by tailors, no clues are available about possible dates, so a certain amount of guesswork becomes necessary. As one of the patterns is marked 'Approved' the inference is that one had previously been accepted

and was about to be updated or modernised. All carry the Earl of Chester's Yeomanry title, indicating a date post 1848, the central design remaining the same in each case, Prince of Wales's feathers and motto 'Ich Dien', below a crown and with a wreath of laurels to left and right. Prices range between 50 to 60 guineas; for the last mentioned price a rose coloured ground in damask would be available although velour would be £3 extra and any new ornaments would add to the price again. It is thought therefore that the obsolete pattern would have had a blue ground and the new, dark red, without ornaments. This pattern seems to be borne out when comparing with the only known photograph of the mounted band on parade with drum horse and drum banners, the picture taken on the racecourse at Chester[3].

The 1890s throw up fresh problems concerning a possible replacement pattern similar to that shown as Illustration No. 7 on our Chart, and cigarette card No. 30. The artist Harry Payne was usually reliable when portraying Cavalry and Yeomanry subjects, but two sketches he made, one dated 1890 and another 1900, show minor differences. The banner he shows is dull red with gold lace edging and fringe, a narrow red line running through the broad lace edging. The Prince of Wales's feather plume is white, the scroll blue with narrow gold edging and lettering but the wreath has been removed and the interwoven letters E C Y C appear at left and right central positions. The Chart denotes title scroll in three sections whilst Payne shows one curved scroll only. His drum horse is grey and he illustrates the small pattern busby, similar to those of Prussian Hussars, a pattern peculiar at this time to the Regiment. The band plume is all red and the busby bag white, the tunic has red collar and cuffs and white braid.

The 1890s probably saw the last phase of the mounted band and the last drum horse about 1900. A 1907 photograph of the band at camp indicates full Hussar dress still in wear, pill-box caps in place of busbies and white band aiguillettes worn from the left shoulders by the 18 bandsmen. Kettle-drums were without covers.

1. *The Earl of Chester's Regiment of Yeomanry Cavalry*: Its formation and services 1797-1897. Ballantyne Press, Edinburgh 1898
2. Sketches of these six patterns kindly supplied by Mr. W. Y. Carman.
3. Reproduced in the *Navy and Army Illustrated* 2 July 1898. Photograph credited to G. Mark Cook.

The Derbyshire Yeomanry Cavalry

During the early years of the Regiment's recorded History[1] there is an interesting note for 3 October 1823. It tells how a silver trumpet was presented by the officers of the Derbyshire Yeomanry Cavalry (1794-1827), to Trumpet-Major Robert Hope, 'who had for 29 years filled that office in the Corps'. One may assume from this statement that there had been some sort of a band of music throughout the whole of this period.

In later years the Regiment could boast a strong band, a photograph of *c.* 1894 shows as many as 31 musicians and bandmaster, whilst another picture of 1905 shows a reduced number, 21, and the bandmaster. Whether the band was ever mounted is not known although a set of drum banners were apparently owned at some time. Johnson relates that the banners were made of crimson cloth with the red and white rose worked in gold thread below the crown — as central design[2]. Both the Chart illustration No. 12 and cigarette card No. 37 add to this a wreath and a title scroll.

The full dress of the Derbyshire Yeomanry during this pre-1914 period was a blue Dragoon uniform with red facings, and white metal helmet with a red and white plume.

[1.] *A Record of the Volunteer Cavalry of Derbyshire, 1794-1864*. By Charles B. Colville.

[2.] Brief notes describing Standards, Guidons and drum banners of the cavalry and the yeomanry in *The Flags of our Fighting Army* by Stanley C. Johnson, pub. 1918 by A. & C. Black Ltd.; as the author quotes one of his sources as Gale & Polden's folders on the subject, one suspects that he has taken his information from these G. & P. Sheets.

DEVONSHIRE

Royal 1st Devon Yeomanry Cavalry

The first reference to a band appears for 1827, but details of uniform, and whether the band was ever mounted at this early date are not known. There is pictorial evidence of the 1840 uniform of a Trumpeter[1] and then by 1863 the *Illustrated London News* (19 September) gives an illustration of the dismounted band at a ceremony at Exeter. By this time the Regiment and band were wearing helmets, introduced in 1852, in conjunction with scarlet Horse Artillery type jackets with blue facings and close chest braid of white piping. In the early 1870s the helmet was replaced by a R.H.A. type busby with red bag and white out of red plume.

It was during the 1870-80 period that the first pictorial evidence of a drum horse appears, a very clear photograph of the mounted drummer, dapple grey drum horse and crimson drum banners (Figs. 5 & 6). The description of the banner is as follows[2]:

Size 39 ins. x 19½ ins., of crimson velvet with 1 inch lace edging at the top and 1¾ ins. gold oakleaf edging at sides and base, a 3 inch gold fringe. The crown is Guelphic pattern, gold embroidery with coiled silver wire pearls, green silk orb, red and green silk jewels and scarlet silk cap. The VR cypher is of gold wire embroidery. The scroll is of blue petersham silk, gold wire embroidery, lettering and edging, the wording: ROYAL 1st DEVON YEOMANRY CAVALRY.

Apparently some time prior to 1914 replacement banners were obtained and were noted at R.H.Q., Dix's Field, Exeter, as late as 1955. The pattern and colouring closely followed the old set although there was a slight variation in the arrangement of the title scroll which appeared in three parts as follows:

ROYAL   CAVALRY
1st DEVON YEOMANRY

Our own illustration, Chart No. 14, is fairly accurate apart from the arrangement of the title wording, a mistake repeated on cigarette card No. 41.

Whilst photographs between 1900-1914 indicate that the Regimental band was much in demand, none shows a mounted band.

[1.] Oil painting by W. Miles of a Trooper and Trumpeter 1840. Reproduced in black and white, J.A.H.R. Vol. XVII, p. 182.

[2.] Fullest details including sketch and colour photograph kindly supplied by the present owner Major Gerald Flint-Shipman.

The Royal North Devon Hussars

Mention has already been made of a drum banner of the Royal 1st Devon Yeomanry at R.H.Q. Exeter. The same H.Q. also had in its possession in 1955, in addition to Regimental Guidons, two different patterns of drum banner, formerly the property of the Royal North Devon Hussars.

The date of formation of the first troop in the northern part of the picturesque county of Devon was May 1798, and after the North Devon Regiment of Yeomanry Cavalry was ordered to disband in 1828, the Regiment served on without pay, was never disbanded and placed back on pay in 1831. The Regimental History[1] tells us that a band was in existence as early as 1829 and in 1835 it is recorded that the Hon. Lady Rolle, wife of the Colonel of the Regiment presented a pair of magnificent drum banners together with four Squadron Standards. In 1842 the band was mounted, the Regiment then under the command of Colonel Clinton.

Sleigh's *List* of 1850 describes the uniform of the North Devon Regiment as follows: Regimental

Fig. 5: Royal 1st Devon Yeomanry c. 1870-80.

7

Appointments — Light Dragoons, silver, uniform blue, facings scarlet, Light Dragoon jacket, scarlet shako, black plume French pattern. Horse appointments same as 14th Light Dragoons with the exception of a panel to the saddle instead of a blanket, and no sheepskin. Strength of band — 16.

In 1853 the Commanding Officer, Sir Trevor Wheler, formerly 16th Lancers, made application to have his corps converted to Mounted Riflemen and this was agreed. There was very little outward sign of change at that time with the exception of the shako and badge. The shako was a tall pattern said to be copied from a type used in Belgium, of scarlet cloth with black plume. (Another specimen of blue is known.) Cap-lines are decorated with a scarlet fleck, the front of shako has a wheel of silver or gold lace, a button in the centre carrying the Regimental badge of crossed carbine and sword, whilst a large metal badge of same design rests above the leather peak. For the uniform of the band however colours were reversed, *i.e.*, with a scarlet jacket. The title Royal was added in 1856 — now the Royal North Devon Mounted Rifles. As by 1868 the Regiment changed to a Hussar Corps with standard blue Hussar uniform, it is possible to date one of the sets of drum banners as between 1856–1868. It is thought that although the title of the Regiment changed and was incorporated on a new set of banners, the old Mounted Rifles set was probably used for field work up to the close of the century. A photograph of the mounted band taken at Barnstaple and reproduced in the *Navy and Army Illustrated* of 16 July 1897, shows this banner in use. It was scarlet with silver border and fringe, had an interwoven silver VR cypher occupying much of the centre ground, but strangely enough had no crown. The title scrolls appeared below in this manner:

DEVON

ROYAL NORTH   MOUNTED RIFLES

Fig. 6: Royal 1st Devon Yeomanry *c.* 1870-80.

Our Fig. 7 shows an interesting Victorian Regimental banner, now in a private collection — the owner has kindly supplied the fullest details about it, together with an accurate drawing. The particulars are as follows: overall width, excluding fringes: 32¾ ins.; maximum depth, excluding fringes: 16¾ ins. The banner is of scarlet cloth, the fringing is blue and silver. The crown is of gold embroidery, with silver pearls, the cap of crimson velvet. The jewels are of silk, red/green/red/green/red. The cypher is of silver wire embroidery, the inserts of gold wire embroidery. The tripartite scroll

Fig. 7: Royal North Devon Hussars *c.* 1890.

Fig. 8: Royal North Devon Hussars. Drum-head service, North Molton, 1913.

is of purple velvet, embroidered in silver wire embroidery ROYAL/NORTH DEVON/HUSSARS. The scroll is edged in silver wire embroidery, the remainder of the scroll work is in skeleton form, traced in silver wire embroidery. It is not entirely certain when this banner would have been in use. It may date from early Victorian days with the possibility of the scrolls showing the title added at some time after 1856.

The old original drums of the North Devon Yeomanry were used at a drum-head service when the Regiment was at its annual camp (Fig. 8), North Molton 1913. One of these drums of painted copper is believed to be amongst Regimental relics of the Royal Devon Yeomanry, now preserved at the T.A. Centre, Barnstaple. A photograph of the drum, together with various other uniform pieces etc., illustrates the Exeter Museum Publication No. 84[3].

[1.] *The Yeomanry of Devon 1794-1927* By Engineer Commander Benson Freeman, R.N., pub. The St. Catherine Press, Stamford Street, London 1927.
[2.] The Yeomanry collection of Major Gerald Flint-Shipman.
[3.] Published by the Royal Albert Museum, Queen Street, Exeter.

The Queen's Own Dorsetshire Yeomanry

During the 1950s this Regiment, then a Field Regiment of Royal Artillery (T.A.), had their early banners of the 1830-37 William IV period, then in a sad condition, restored. The original ground was apparently crimson in colour, called mauve before restoration, probably much faded, but restored to a bright scarlet. The original separate pieces had been skilfully replaced and consisted of the following: At the top and bottom two scrolls of royal blue material with the Regimental title QUEEN'S OWN at the top and REGIMENT OF YEOMANRY CAVALRY on a long continuous scroll at the bottom, lettering described as of silver but more likely of worn gold. The approximate size of banner 40 ins. x 18 ins., on either side of central device a wreath of oakleaves in gold embroidery, an embroidered crown in the centre between and above a reversed W R cypher, with the numerals IV below. The banner surrounded with gold thread fringe[1].

From as early a date as 1833 feelers had been put out by the officers that the Regiment be honoured with a Royal title, so after escort duty for H.R.H. The Duchess of Kent an official application was made, and promptly turned down by Whitehall. However, a further application in 1843 was successful when H.M. The Queen was graciously pleased to approve the title of The 'Queen's Own' Regiment of Yeomanry Cavalry. One assumes that this title was added to the existing drum banners and will explain how a 'Queen's Own' title appeared on William IV banners.

Between 1844 and the 1860s there were a number of changes made in uniform and it is also likely that sometime during this period new drum banners were acquired. (By the 1860s the Regiment had a fine band and in 1861 and 1863, under Bandmaster Eyers, took first prize on both occasions at the Crystal Palace.) The artist R. Simkin made a pleasing watercolour of a dismounted officer and the mounted kettle-drummer on the drum horse of 1873[2]. In this year pantaloons were introduced for mounted parades, blue with two white stripes and worn in conjunction with butcher boots; the tunic of dark blue with scarlet collar and cuffs and with three white cords of Hussar braiding on chest. For headgear the low French style kepi (or shako) with white hair plume, the kettle-drummer's uniform as described but with a scarlet plume. (In 1881 the uniform was changed into that of an Hussar Corps and the black Hussar busbies with red busby bags and white plumes and lines, replaced the shako. An additional three loops of Hussar braiding on the chest was finally added in 1885.) In Simkin's picture the drum horse is a grey, the drum banners of simple design, almost exactly as shown in the Chart No. 27, and on the cigarette card No. 38.

In 1885 Captain Montague Guest, M.P., presented to the officers a cigar box with a beautifully decorated lid showing uniforms, etc., and in one of the vignettes a kettle-drum and drum banner, details of the latter agreeing with our illustration. This valuable gift was handed over in the 1950s for safe keeping to the County Museum, Dorchester.

It is unlikely that the band was ever mounted during the Edwardian years.

1. Mr. W. Y. Carman inspected these banners and kindly supplied me with full details at the time.
2. One of the 13 watercolours used to illustrate the *Records of the Dorset Imperial Yeomanry 1894-1905*, Vol. II Edited by Captain M. F. Gage; 1906.

The Hampshire Yeomanry (Carabiniers)

The Yeomanry of the county, formed about 1794, was soon to be known as the Northern and Southern Yeomanry Cavalry corps respectively, but splintered into many Troops. The Southern corps retained its identity until c. 1850, then was absorbed by the North Hampshire, c. 1853 and now entitled The Hampshire Yeomanry. Records tell us that the South Hampshire had a band as early as 1808, but that a mounted band was formed by the North Hampshire c. 1835. A picture of a dismounted band appeared in the *Illustrated London News* of 25 January 1845, performing during a visit by Her Majesty to Strathfieldsaye, the Hampshire seat of the Duke of Wellington. A newspaper account of 1861 mentions the band 'having an able, youthful drummer, a young man of colour'.

In 1884 the Hon. H. G. L. Crichton was appointed to command and within a few years had reorganised the corps. Based on his long service with regular cavalry he turned the Regiment into a highly efficient Yeomanry Cavalry corps, and gradually standardised dress, mainly following that of his former regiment, the 6th Dragoon Guards. A fine print dated 1887[1] shows the various patterns of dress for all ranks, and includes a vignette of the mounted band with the first known drum banners. These are of simple but effective design, blue with silver fringe all round, a crown in full colours, the interwoven letters 'H Y C' and the white rose between. Band horses are greys, the drum horse a skewbald, and there are apparently 14 musicians. Uniforms at this date consisted of a white metal helmet without plume, blue frock without facing colour, white piping round tunic, on collar and cuffs and back seams, also double white stripes on blue pantaloons. In 1894 red hair plumes were provided for the band and white for the remainder of the Regiment, but not worn in marching-order. A photograph of the late 1880s show a mounted band of 12 plus bandmaster, horses of mixed colours, uniform as described, kettle-drums not covered but the drum casings carry the old title $\frac{N\,H}{Y\,C}$, as well as an elaborate trophy of arms painted upon them.

More banners were acquired about 1887 when the Hampshire Carabiniers title was officially conferred. These were deep blue in colour, 58 ins. long, 24 ins. deep and with a one inch band of white material all round. The central design consisted of a white metal crown above the Carabiniers crest, *i.e.*, a white metal rose encircled by a garter with the title CARABINIERS over crossed carbines and the words HAMPSHIRE YEOMANRY on a scroll below, all lettering in silver thread and there are two edgings of narrow silver lace around the cypher.

It is possible that this design of drum banner was an interim pattern, as during the 1890s a splendid pair of ornate banners were obtained. These were slightly smaller than the former, 43 ins. long and 21 ins. deep, edged with two bands of ¾ inch gold lace with a white line running through and gold fringe all round, again deep blue in colour. The Chart illustration No. 28 and the cigarette card No. 36 are both fair representations, although the roses are actually of gold embroidery with red centres. Both patterns of banner are now preserved at the Royal Hampshire Regiment's Museum at Winchester.

Between 1887 and 1897 the Regiment used as many as four different horses at various times to carry the kettle-drums. A photograph of the mounted band[2] of the mid-90s shows an all-white drum horse and mixed colours for band horses, the new drum banners in use. Another photograph taken at some near date shows a drum horse of two colours, whilst a picture taken at camp between 1899 and 1901 shows an all-black drum horse[3]. In this latest picture the kettle-drummer wears a blue serge frock, white gorget patches on collar and steel shoulder chains. It is known that the mounted band was maintained up to 1900-01 but whether it so remained after this date is very doubtful.

1. Reproduced on back cover.
2. Published in a periodical called *The Million*, 1897.
3. Published in *The Regiment*, 16 November 1901.

The Queen's Own West Kent Yeomanry

The Regimental Museum at Hever Castle, which displays the memorabilia of both the former Kent Yeomanry regiments, is able to show two pairs of drum banners for the West Kent Yeomanry.

The West Kent regiment was also fortunate to have had in its ranks one of the most popular military artists of the day, Harry Payne, who served from 1883 to 1906 with the Regiment[1]. When the Regimental History[2] came to be produced therefore, an excellent artist was on hand to paint six of the colour plates covering uniforms worn between 1801 and 1907.

Very little is recorded about the band prior to the turn of the century so we are unable to tell when the earlier banners were used, suffice to say they were comparatively plain but at the same time of the most attractive design (Fig. 9). The size was 21 ins. x 40 ins., colour black but with silver lace edging and fringe, the prancing White Horse of Kent as central motif, scarlet scrolls with edging and wording of silver thread[3]. There are no known photographs showing the banners in

Fig. 9: Q.O. West Kent Yeomanry. Date not known, probably 1880s.

actual use, but there is one of interest which may have been taken in 1888 when both Kent regiments were brigaded at Maidstone and inspected by the Duke of Cambridge. The mounted band of the West Kent Yeomanry is in the foreground, its drum horse in front. This horse has no throat plume or special furniture, bandsmen are in undress — pill-box caps, blue stable jackets with red collars and cuffs, white piping and double white stripes on the blue pantaloons. A large metal badge can be seen (on red cloth backing) mounted on the flap of one of the white music pouches. On the left flank of the West Kent can be seen Mounted Riflemen from East Kent in their all-green uniforms.

Harry Payne made preliminary sketches of the drum horse, scarlet banners and showing the rider in blue Hussar uniform, the drummer said to be a Corporal J. Lower of 26 Earl Street, Maidstone, the painting drawn from life *c.* 1887, but unfortunately the finished work was never published. The Hussar busby has a red bag and white out of red brush plume from a white boss, the busby lines and body lines are red and white. The blue review order tunic has five loops of white chest braid, collar and cuffs of scarlet and double white stripes on pantaloons. Payne notes that the drum horse has an ordinary bridle and head collar, there is no throat plume or shabraque.

The details of the drum banner, Chart No. 24, is not accurate although improved upon on cigarette card No. 44, where the wording on cypher and title scrolls had been corrected. The size of the drum banner, which is in splendid condition, is 21 ins. x 41 ins.

A battle honour for 'SOUTH AFRICA. 1900-01' was awarded in 1904, but not added to the banner until the 1920s when the principal battle honours for World

War 1 were added, making three on each side of the wreath (Fig. 10).

1. See *For Queen and Country: The Career of Harry Payne Military Artist 1858-1927.* By Michael Cane. Privately printed 1977.
2. *The West Kent (Queen's Own) Yeomanry: Some Historical Records 1794-1909.* Lieut.-Colonel J. F. Edmeades, M.V.O. Pub. Andrew Melrose, London 1909.
3. I am most grateful to Boris Mollo for colour photographs and descriptions of the drum banners, and indeed for much help regarding the Kent Regiments.

The Queen's Own Royal Glasgow Yeomanry

A regiment raised in 1797 was known as the Glasgow Light Horse, but was disbanded in 1814, although it is said that the Glasgow Troop was never formally disbanded — but just dwindled away. A new regiment was re-raised in 1848 with the title Glasgow and Lower Ward of Lanarkshire Yeomanry Cavalry the 'Queen's Own' Royal title conferred in 1849 after Queen Victoria, H.R.H. Prince Albert and the royal children had paid a visit to the city on 14 August, and the Regiment successfully performed escort duty. The Regimental History[1] tells us that from the very start the Glasgow Yeomanry could boast a fine mounted band, 'which added greatly to the gaiety at parades and inspections'. Five years later the city commemorated the 1849 visit by erecting an equestrian statue of Her Majesty in St. Vincent Place. At the unveiling ceremony, and subsequent procession, the mounted band 'performed amidst the waving of hats and handkerchiefs'. A picture in the *Illustrated London News* of 16 September 1854 shows a section of the band and the mounted kettle-drummer, but no banners are in evidence.

Fig. 10: Q.O. West Kent Yeomanry. Date not known, probably late 1890s.

Other pictorial evidence of the mounted band from then on seems to be non-existent although the Regimental History states that in 1887 when Queen Victoria celebrated her Jubilee, and in honour of this event, there was a military review in June on the Green, and that for the march past the band of the Yeomanry rode into the centre of the ground and struck up 'The Garb of Old Gaul'. Every year from then on there was always a mounted parade in Blytheswood Square before marching to Hamilton to camp, up till the South African War.

Drum banners were eventually acquired (Fig. 11) and kept at R.H.Q. (believed Yorkhill Parade), but they seem to be in such good condition one wonders if they were ever used. It can be seen that both the Chart No. 19

illustration, and cigarette card No. 33 are fairly good representations with correct colouring.

1. *The Queen's Own Royal Glasgow Yeomanry, 1848-1948.* Printed for the Regiment by Robert Maclehose & Co. Ltd., University Press, Glasgow, 1949.

LANCASHIRE

The Lancashire Hussars

This Regiment was raised in 1848 by Sir John Gerard, Bt., and before his death in February 1854 was up to full strength, three Troops, equipped and uniformed as Hussars. Sir John was succeeded by his brother Robert Tolver Gerard as 13th Baronet and Major-Commandant

Fig. 11: Q.O. Royal Glasgow Yeomanry. Date not known, probably late 1880s.

of the Regiment; Sir Robert was created Baron Gerard in 1876.

The artist John Ferneley Jnr. was commissioned, probably by Sir Robert, to record the appearance of the Regiment on parade, which he did in fine style by completing two magnificent oil paintings. One of these was sold at auction in July 1987 and purchased by the Regiment[1], the picture showing Sir Robert and his Trumpeter in the foreground and the whole Regiment parading with the mounted band just visible on the right flank. The other painting[2], again with Sir Robert inspecting the Regiment, is from an opposite angle showing the band in a foremost position. With the exception of the plume which is red for Trumpeters and all bandsmen, the uniform is the same for the remainder of the Regiment, i.e., crimson shako with black plume, blue jacket with close gold or yellow (according to rank) chest braid covering the whole of the front, piping, cuffs, etc., and trousers with similar gold/yellow stripe. All ranks have blue shabraques edged crimson vandykes, leopardskin saddle covers for officers, black sheepskin for other ranks, gold and crimson faced sabretaches for officers.

The band is mounted on greys and would appear to be about 15 strong, the large drum banners are crimson with probably gold ornamentation.

It is known that new silver drums were presented by Captain W. Gerard (later Colonel Lord Gerard, D.S.O.), and Lieutenant L. Walmesley in May 1882, and it is probable that new drum banners were obtained at the same time. The date of presentation, and the names of donors of the drums are inscribed on the shell(s), whilst in addition, as gilt mounts on the shells, a Queen's crown, a Lancaster rose and a title scroll are affixed. The crown has crimson enamel cushions, the rose has some green and gold ornamentation whilst the scroll and letters, LANCASHIRE HUSSARS are gilt. Both the drums and banners are still in the Regiment's possession.

Our illustration, Chart No. 18 (and also cigarette card No. 49), would appear to be very close in detail to the original — crimson ground, Royal Cypher interlaced, surmounted by crown and Lancastrian rose below, surrounded by a wreath of roses, shamrock and thistles. The Regimental title is on a blue scroll at the foot of the banner[3].

By 1882 of course the Regiment was clothed as Hussars, uniform blue with silver lace or white braid, Hussar busby with crimson bag and white out of crimson plume, all crimson for band and Trumpeters.

A mounted band was maintained up to 1908 and was photographed at Delamere, bandsmen then wearing blue serge tunics with crimson collars and cuffs, chains on shoulders etc., overalls with white stripes, peaked staff caps of crimson. The band horses of mixed colouring, the drum horse a grey, drums uncovered. It would appear that drum banners were (very wisely) left at H.Q. on these annual occasions, which probably accounts for the lack of photographs showing both drums and banners.

One cannot leave this Regiment without mention of its famous Bandmaster from 1871-1914 (or even until 1922), Mr. Thomas Batley, brother of George Batley who was the equally renowned Bandmaster of the Duke of Lancaster's Own Yeomanry. He, Thomas, lived near R.H.Q., Prince Alfred Road, Liverpool, also Depot for the band and signallers. He received his I.Y. Long Service and Good Conduct Medal in July 1905. He played cornet with the band, riding in the front rank at offside position when mounted, or if dismounted preferring to march at the rear.

He was photographed, still as Bandmaster at camp at Rufford in 1914, but he may even have continued until 1922, thereby maintaining the family record of 50 years band service. He died at Manchester in 1939 aged 93.

1. Reproduced as a black and white plate in J.A.H.R. Vol. XL, p.196, together with an article by Major A. McK. Annand. The Regiment reproduced the painting in colour as a Christmas card.
2. Present whereabouts not known.
3. Detail supplied by R. J. Smith after close inspection in 1981 and we are also grateful to Captain R. Koss, Lancashire Hussars, for kindly photographing the drum banners at R.H.Q.,

The Duke of Lancaster's Own Yeomanry

There is reference to a Regimental band in 1838, but by 1846 it is recorded that a mounted band was formed[1]. It was in that year that the Regiment was fortunate enough to obtain the services of a former Trumpet-Major of the 2nd Life Guards. William Henry Batley who had retired in 1845 after 32 years service joined the Worsley Troop the following year, retiring from the Regiment in 1867, thus having served for 50 years[2]. At the tender age of 14 Batley's son George joined the Duke of Lancaster's Own band as a solo cornet player, and we are told that at his age had to be lifted up on to his horse. He, George, became a Trumpeter in 1867 and was eventually appointed Bandmaster in 1884, a position he held until retirement in 1898[3].

New drum banners were presented to the Regiment in 1899 by two Regimental officers, Major P. Hargraves and Major W. C. Jones. The reproduction, Chart No. 30, is a reliable picture, as is the cigarette card No. 32. The central design on the dark blue banner is a red shield with the three lions of England surcharged with a white label or bar, having three points. Above is an imperial crown, a laurel wreath to the left of shield and an oakleaf on the right, a triple scroll carries the Regimental title THE DUKE OF — LANCASTER'S — YEOMANRY. The red rose ensigned by a coronet appears in the two lower corners. Fig. 12 shows the drum banner after 1902 when the 'South Africa 1900-1902' battle honour was added[4].

Prior to 1899 the drum banners, last seen at a mounted parade on Southport sands on 27 May 1898, were also blue with gold fringe, a central design below a crown and with, apparently, short sprays left and right

1. A complete section dealing with the Regimental band appears in Booklet No. 6 in the A.M.O.T. Series of Uniforms of the British Yeomanry Forces 1794-1914. Pub. 1983.
2. W. H. Batley was selected in 1832 as the subject for a study by A. J. Dubois Drahonet. Illustration No. 2106 in Military Drawings and Paintings in the Royal Collection by A. E. Haswell Miller and N. P. Dawnay. Phaidon 1966.
3. An account of his career published in The Yeomanry Record of May 1898.
4. Illustrated in colour, A.M.O.T. Booklet No. 6.

Fig. 12: Duke of Lancaster's Own Yeomanry. Presented 1899.

below. Band horses were greys, the last drum horse a piebald, possibly skewbald, having a scarlet throat plume. In mounted review order the bandsmen were distinguished by red helmet plumes and yellow plaited band aiguillettes worn from the left shoulder. A photograph of the mounted band at the 1903 camp shows that slouch hats were worn by bandsmen on this occasion and that drum banners were not used. It is quite possible that this may have been the last turnout as a mounted band.

LONDON

The City of London Yeomanry (Rough Riders)

The Rough Riders was one of the new regiments formed during the South Africa War and dates from 18 July 1901. It was accepted as the 20th Bn. Imperial Yeomanry, and took its title Rough Riders from a body of volunteer horsemen who fought under Colonel Theodore Roosevelt in the Spanish-American War of 1898. It was able to raise four Companies for service in South Africa, subsequently awarded the battle-honour 'SOUTH AFRICA 1900-02'. The Regiment's first Commanding Officer was Colonel Viscount Maitland, an officer with much experience in the regular army and who had served in South Africa as Adjutant of the 20th I.Y.

He ignored the order that the Regiment should be dressed in khaki and introduced a most attractive uniform, the colour initially styled Austrian blue but later to be known as French grey, at first with purple collar and cuffs; eventually for review order a purple

plastron was added[1]. A large proportion of the NCOs and men in the 1902 regiment had served in South Africa so within a short time the new City of London Yeomanry had earned a reputation for efficiency and smartness.

A Regimental band was raised and appeared on several occasions during 1903; at some time in the summer months a photograph shows this small band, mounted on greys, riding through Hyde Park. The bandsmen wear the French grey uniform in conjunction with slouch hats; the kettle-drums have no drum banners at that time. In November 1903 it is recorded that the mounted band rode in the Lord Mayor's Procession; as the weather was wet the band was cloaked. Drum banners did appear on this occasion, they were of plain purple material without any crest or ornamentation but with a broad gold edging and gold fringe. The artist Harry Payne was able to paint a picture of the kettle-drummer at this time, but his painting does however show one or two minor errors in that the purple cuffs should be pointed lancer cuffs and not with yellow edging and Austrian knots, and similarly the cap-lines should be purple, not yellow as shown. In 1906 the band, performing at the Mansion House wore lancer dress with peaked caps; lance-caps as such were not worn by the rank and file although several officers possessed them.

It is thought that about this time more elaborate banners were obtained, again purple with gold lace edging and fringe but with the addition of the City Arms as central design worked in silver, scarlet and gold, with an oakleaf wreath in green surrounding the crest. Chart

No. 17 shows a fair representation of the banner at this stage although it is believed that there was no broad band of French grey surrounding as shown, but French grey piping separating the purple cloth from the gold edging.

In June 1909 the dismounted band in lancer dress led the Regiment, together with the other City corps, through the City on a recruiting march[2] but later that year the mounted band took part as usual in the Lord Mayor's Procession. A photograph was published showing the band in lancer full dress, less lance-caps, and mounted on greys[3].

After the Great War the Regiment's 10 battle-honours (in addition to 'SOUTH AFRICA 1900-02' which had always occupied a separate scroll at the foot of the banner) were worked on to separate scrolls mounted upon the wreath. In addition, at top right position the Regimental badge, the letters R R upon a spur, was embroidered on the banner, whilst at top left position the badge of the Machine Gun Corps was also added — the 1st City of London Yeomanry, together with the 1st/3rd County of London Yeomanry, became part of the Machine Gun Corps during the concluding months of the War (Fig. 13).

It is pleasant to know that the distinctive uniform of the Rough Riders can still be seen to this day when worn by the band of the Inns of Court and City Yeomanry, The Royal Yeomanry.

[1.] Photographs of the uniforms at the time of the raising of the Regiment are to be found in the *Navy & Army Illustrated,* 28 February 1903.
[2.] Photograph reproduced in the *Army & Navy Chronicle* of June 1909.
[3.] Photograph reproduced in *The Sphere* of 13 November 1909.

The Middlesex Yeomanry

It was to be about 12 years after the re-raising of the Regiment in 1830 that a band was first formed, this was a brass band of 13 musicians. Much later the Regiment and its band received a mention in *The Times* of 1 June 1843, following an inspection by the Commanding Officer of the 13th Light Dragoons who found — 'the appearance and condition of the Uxbridge Yeomanry highly pleasing and with its new brass band, a very attractive Corps of Yeomanry Cavalry'. In 1872 the Light Dragoon uniform was changed and the Corps adopted Hussar dress, green tunic with black collars and cuffs, yellow lace but only three rows of Hussar braid on chest, later increased to six, double red stripes on overalls; a Hussar busby with dark green bag and a green out of red brush plume. In 1881 the band was mounted on greys.

A drawing by Corbould, published in the *Illustrated London News* of 25 November 1882, gives the first indication of the drum horse. The Regiment provided 10 officers and 130 rank and file to keep the ground at Horse Guards when troops returning from the Egyptian Campaign were welcomed home, the mounted band was on parade. The drum horse is shown between two mounted Troopers, the caption reads ' a drum in leading strings'. The drum banner, as shown in the sketch is plain, but with the Regimental crest, a Star, worked in the centre, and with a double lace border around the cloth, no fringe.

A month before this event however, Sunday 22 October was an important day in band history and is recorded thus in the Regimental History[1]:

'The band of the Regiment paraded in mounted review order, under Bandmaster Graves, at Knightsbridge, and after a minute inspection by Major Tritton proceeded to Knightsbridge Barracks where they were joined by the band of the 1st Life Guards. The two bands then moved off to the docks, where they were further augmented by the band of the Royal Horse Guards, and had the honour of playing the 1st Life Guards, on their return from the Egyptian Campaign, through London to their barracks where the gallant bandsmen were inspected by H.R.H. The Prince of Wales, accompanied by the Princess of Wales, the Princesses Louise, Victoria and Maud, and H.R.H. The Duke of Cambridge. The special wish of the band of the Middlesex Yeomanry to join in this public welcoming of the returned troopers was only natural when the band, without exception at this time, from the Bandmaster downwards were all ex-Household Cavalry men. The band, under Bandmaster Graves, was not only remarkably well mounted, but was considered one of the best bands of the Metropolitan Auxiliary Regiments.'

Fig. 13: Rough Riders *c.* 1906. But with postwar addition of Machine Gun Corps crest. The City of London Yeomanry continues to exist as part of 68 Inns of Court & City Yeomanry Signal Squadron at Stone Buildings, Lincoln's Inn.

Sometime later a pair of very fine drum banners were obtained, a description found under an 1890 entry in Stonham's History, and a close inspection of an original banner, still in Regimental possesion in 1955, is as follows:

'Of dark green plush material, 4ft 3½ ins. x 2ft 2½ ins. size, edged with two borders of ¾ inch gold, narrow black band appearing between the gold, gold fringe of 1½ ins. around banner and on the inside of the lower edge of the top gold band. The central design consists of the Regimental Star surmounted by a crown, enclosed within a laurel wreath. The Star is mounted on scarlet backing cloth, has the motto "PRO ARIS ET FOCIS" (translated by old soldiers as — "For 'ares and foxes") and the title MIDDLESEX YEOMANRY on the cypher, and VR within. In the top left and bottom right corners are the interwoven letters of the title MYC and the date, 1830, in the opposite corners. It will be seen therefore that both the Chart illustration No. 26 and cigarette card No. 40 differ in numerous ways, mainly the colour of the banner too light, corner decorations incorrect and a few other small minor variations.'

A fine drawing of the mounted kettle-drummer, by A. Roberson who was a Sergeant in the Regiment, was published in the magazine *The Regiment*. One of the occasional mounted parades of the 1890s when the band paraded with the Regiment in Hyde Park was photographed and reproduced in the *Navy & Army Illustrated* of 9 April 1897, the band still mounted on greys. In November 1899 the mounted band performed at the Lord Mayor's Show but there are no references to mounted parades after this date, although the Regiment still maintained a fine band. It is interesting to recall that, certainly during the 1960s and 70s, a dismounted band of the successor Regiment (Signals) was often to be seen at the Cavalry Memorial Parades in Hyde Park.

[1.] *Historical Records of the Middlesex Yeomanry: 1797-1927* by Charles Stonham and Benson Freeman. Pub. by the Regimental Committee, Duke of York's H.Q., Chelsea, 1930.

3rd County of London Yeomanry (Sharpshooters)
Another London regiment, originally formed for service in South Africa as part of an Imperial Yeomanry battalion, eventually provided men for the 18th I.Y. Bn., then later for 21st and 23rd Bns. The name 'Sharpshooters' was one which proved popular in 1899 so subsequently in 1901, when the Earl of Dunraven applied for permission to raise a Regiment of Yeomanry for home service, sanctioned in June 1901, he could not better the title which had earned such respect in South Africa — Sharpshooters. By 1902 nearly a third of the strength of the new Regiment wore South Africa medals.

A former Trooper in the Regiment who served as a Medical Officer (R.A.M.C.) throughout the 1914-18 War, told a delightful story about Lord Dunraven's initial choice of uniform. His idea was to have a white Hussar uniform. 'A Sergeant in this striking dress was sent to Buckingham Palace so that King Edward might inspect it. His Majesty asked the Sergeant "Did people stare at you?" and received the reply, "No Sir. I was wearing my overcoat!"' Of course, the final choice was an attractive Hussar dress of more tasteful and sober colours, thus described in the Regimental History[1].

'Full dress 1901-14. As worn by regular Hussar Regiments except it was green with gold lace. The busby had a dark green bag and a yellow plume with green base. In February 1909 the colour of the uniform was changed to a darker shade of green and the plume became all white. Officers wore a gold crossbelt with primrose train and silver pickers, buckles and pouch; after the award of the battle-honour "SOUTH AFRICA 1900-02" a silver slide was added to the crossbelt. The soldier's uniform was similar to that of the officers except that yellow cord replaced gold lace.'

A band was formed during the early days and served up to 1914, both dismounted and mounted, photos of the dismounted band of c. 1904 are known and reproduced in the A.M.O.T. Yeomanry Booklet[2]. The same book describes the circumstances concerning a drum banner, *i.e.*, that shown and illustrated on Chart No. 16: 'In 1914 drum banners were designed by Trooper Coventry, an amateur artist serving in the Sharpshooters, in order that the design could be included in a folder of *Yeomanry Guidons and Drum Banners* which was later produced by Gale & Polden; but it is thought that no drum banners were actually made, for a photograph of the band, mounted, in 1914, shows only the plain copper kettle-drum shells'.

[1.] *The Sharpshooters: 3rd County of London Yeomanry 1900-1961, Kent and County of London Yeomanry 1961-1970.* By Boris Mollo. Pub. Historical Research Unit, 1970.

[2.] *The Uniforms of the British Yeomanry Force 1794-1914.* No. 5. *3rd County of London (Sharpshooters)* by L. Barlow and R. J. Smith. Pub. A.M.O.T. 1983. Photographs and descriptions of all known uniforms and badges between 1900 and 1914 included in this book.

The Lothian and Border Horse
In 1797 three regiments were raised in the Lowlands of Scotland, namely — The Berwickshire Yeomanry Cavalry 1797-1827, The Royal Midlothian Yeomanry Cavalry, 1797-1871, and The East Lothian Yeomanry Cavalry. The last named was actually disbanded in 1827 although one troop remained until 1838, but in 1846 a new regiment was re-raised, with a troop added in 1879 to represent the old Midlothian Yeomanry. The Regiment was re-named in 1888 with the title — Lothians and Berwickshire Yeomanry Cavalry.

This Regiment adopted a uniform styled after the Life Guards, a Heavy Dragoon helmet of white metal with gilt ornaments, white helmet plume (red for band), but instead of a tunic a scarlet waist-jacket with blue collar and cuffs edged with gold lace. Shoulder scales were attached to the jacket; pantaloons and overalls were blue, two broad scarlet stripes with a narrow scarlet welt between, again similar to those of the Life Guards. Apart from the scarlet helmet plume bandsmen were further distinguished by four broad gold lace bars on the front of the jacket.

Bandmaster R. S. Farquharson, a Crimean veteran of the 4th Light Dragoons who had ridden in the Charge, took over the band in 1888 on his transfer from the Ayrshire Yeomanry.

In the late 1880s and 1890s the Regiment was renowned for its Musical Ride, accompanied by appropriate music from the band. The riders carried lances so there was some justification for one of the Regiment's nicknames — The Princes Street Lancers.

The drum banners probably date from the late 1880s when the official title was changed. The new full title appeared around the garter — LOTHIANS AND BERWICKSHIRE with the words YEOMANRY CAVALRY on a separate scroll below, and the initials

L B Y C below a crown at either side of the banner. On a photograph taken during the late 1890s the thistle flowers of silver and the silver sheaf of wheat badge, or garb, within the garter, shows up against the dark blue cloth. A special shabraque, also of blue with a broad gold edging and with similar design on hind sections, was used — also a scarlet throat-plume and there was an ornamental head-harness for the grey drum horse (Fig. 14). Another photo of the same period shows a small mounted band, all on greys. The illustration, Chart No. 20 and cigarette card No. 48 are both reasonably accurate.

By the time of the next change of title, 1908, there had also been some changes in dress and equipment. The full dress had been altered by the substitution of the jacket for a scarlet Dragoon tunic with blue shoulder straps instead of the scales, blue collars and with blue gauntlet cuffs, similar to the Household Cavalry. The band retained their scarlet helmet plumes but there had been a change of drum banner. At a Royal Review, Edinburgh, the mounted band and a Guard of Honour marched through Princes Street wearing the new tunics and displaying the new banners. The latter were scarlet with gold border and fringe, the central design being the Royal Arms embroidered in full colours with the motto — DIEU — ET MON — DROIT on a triple scroll below. There were green thistle sprays on each corner and the initials L B H below a crown, on either side of the banners in a central position.

Fig. 14: Lothians and Border Horse. Date not known, taken in Edinburgh *c.* 1890s.

The Montgomeryshire Yeomanry
There appears to be no recorded date concerning the formation of a band in this Regiment, although what is most unusual is that we find the presentation and description of the Regiment's first (probably the only) pair of drum banners is fully recorded.

'The 1851 training, which was held as usual at headquarters, and began on May 12th, was made the occasion of the presentation by the Viscountess Seaham of a pair of gorgeous kettle-drum banners to the band of the Regiment, adding to the value of her gift by addressing a few words to the Regiment, in which this year Viscount Seaham, 1st Life Guards, had accepted a Captaincy. The banners were of crimson plush, having a thistle, rose, and shamrock, surmounted by a crown; beneath the wreath were two black scrolls, one inscribed with the Regimental motto, and the other the Regimental title in gold, beautifully worked in the centre. In two of the corners were shown the red dragon, on a black field, and in the other two a white horse on a green mount; the drum banners being an exact copy of the Queen's or Royal Standard of the Regiment. The banners were heavily fringed with gold lace.[1]

Sleigh gives band strength in 1850 as 19.

Prior to 1866 the Regiment wore Heavy Dragoon uniform, scarlet with black facings, styled after the 7th Dragoon Guards. There was a complete change however in 1866 to a hybrid uniform, half Dragoon, half Hussar. The headdress was the Hussar busby with red bag and white out of red plume, the tunic scarlet with black collar and cuffs, silver lace for officers, white for rank and file, etc. The band had a special dress: Scarlet brushes to their busbies, the kettle-drummer having three rows of white Hussar braiding.

R. Simkin, who had been commissioned to make a series of seven watercolours as plates for Wynn's Regimental History, chose a mounted kettle-drummer and a dismounted officer as subjects for the uniforms of 1866. Our illustrations, Chart No. 21 and cigarette card No. 47, are, in the main, similar to Simkin's painting, but whereas both the Chart and card show a triple title scroll, Simkin has but one, a long curved scroll carrying the county title only — MONTGOMERYSHIRE; the crowns differ on all three illustrations.

In 1882 the Hussar busby was replaced by a white metal Dragoon helmet without plume, although a white one was later introduced. Most photographs show a dismounted band and it is unlikely to have been mounted after the Boer War years. An exact date is not known but under an entry for 1908 the History records: 'The band for the past few years has not been mounted. The standards, which are now unfortunately not even carried on ceremonial parade, are still in possession at headquarters (Welshpool), where the old drum banners are also stored.'

[1]. *The Historical Records of the Yeomanry and Volunteers of Montgomeryshire, 1803-1908.* Compiled by Lt. Colonel R. W. Williams Wynn, D.S.O., and Benson Freeman, Esq., R.N.R. Pub. Woodall, Minshall, Thomas & Co., Caxton Press, 1909.

The Northumberland Hussars
The Regimental Museum have some very fine reminders of the mounted band of this celebrated Yeomanry corps, the first being a painting of the drum horse of *c.* 1854, a tall handsome grey called 'Mettle'. It is a stable scene before the drums have been assembled, but showing a throat plume in wear, white out of a dark colour, presumably blue, and with a black lambskin saddle-cover. The mounted band of the 1890s is the subject of a spirited painting showing the return from a General Inspection on the Town Moor. All troops on this important parade wear mounted review order, blue Hussar uniform with white (or silver) braid, scarlet busby bag with white out of red busby plume, band uniform similar to the remainder of the regiment. The

Fig. 15: Northumberland Hussars. Lt. H. G. Amers. Bandmaster in the mounted review order of pre-1914.

1895 by the younger Harry Amers, then 17 years of age and the youngest Bandmaster in Britain (Fig, 15). During the years before 1914 he took the band to Belgium, to the U.S.A., and also made several tours in Germany playing in all the big cities and receiving from the Germans the highest acclaim. He served with the Regiment during 1914-18 in France and was commissioned Lieutenant in 1915, invalided in 1919 with rank of Captain.

1. A photograph in the Regimental History, *The History of the Northumberland (Hussars) Yeomanry 1819-1919*; by H. Pease. Constable & Co. Ltd., 1924.

NOTTINGHAMSHIRE

The Sherwood Rangers

The first of the Nottinghamshire regiments is the Sherwood Rangers, an old established regiment dating from 1794, and one rich with historical memorabilia, uniform pieces as well as pictorial and photographic records. It is fairly certain that the Regiment possessed a band, probably mounted, from an early date, but we have to wait until 1885 for pictorial evidence when a photograph shows the entire Regiment on parade in mounted review order — a magnificent spectacle, the mounted band is on the right flank. Unfortunately the kettle-drums are without banners. (This was also the case in December 1898 when a photograph of the kettle-drummer and drum horse was published in a magazine devoted to the Yeomanry — *The Yeomanry Record*.)

Drum banners may have been obtained in 1894 at the same time as the Standard for the Retford Troop was presented by Viscountess Galway. The design and pattern of these banners was quite unique and was seen

drum horse and all band horses are greys, there are no drum banners or horse throat plumes. The Museum also has a pair of George IV Standards, a Drum-Major's staff which was presented in 1865, and a pair of drum banners[1].

Both illustrations, Chart No. 10 and cigarette card No. 34, are correct inasmuch as indicating a very dark shade of blue cloth and a single long scarlet scroll carrying the Regimental title NORTHUMBERLAND HUSSARS (without THE), gold lace edging is 1¾ ins. Irish wave lace and there is a 2 ins. gold fringe; however, little else appears to be correct. The cypher is much more complex and skilfully interwoven than shown, the laurel sprays are wrongly positioned and the shape of the crown is incorrect.

In conclusion one must record that the name of the band of the Northumberland Hussars before 1914 became famous throughout the world. Apart from attracting a succession of skilled musicians to its ranks, ultimate credit must go to the Amers family. Three generations of this musical family served the band, the senior, Harry, becoming a Band Sergeant with 30 years' service, succeeded by his son John Hall Amers who eventually became Bandmaster, and followed in turn in

Fig. 16: Sherwood Rangers. Detail of mounted band with drum horse. Retford 1907.

18

DRUM BANNER. SOUTH NOTTS YEOMANRY.

(Drawn from the actual banner in 1926. by B.T.A. Griffiths.)

1

Fig. 17: South Notts. Hussars. Drawing of 1926 for plate in Regimental History showing drum banner of 1890s.

8

2

3

Lace and fringe. Actual size. Same design on narrow lace at top. All yellow silk. (Note the thread lines are upright except at X, where they are horizontal.)

The V.R. cypher is all yellow silk. and almost entirely bordered with yellow silk roping - single. The crown has crimson silk cap (bit of the dk. blue ground shows in the open corner). Green orb with white "cross", and bordered yellow. Ermine base white with usual black ticks. Jewels on hoops - white, on the head band the centre and side ones are red. The two round ones blue. small ones white. The three crosses outlined red. All the rest is yellow silk.

7

Scroll is the dark blue ground of the banner, bordered yellow silk - double roped. The ends all yellow, being filled in with broken lines of yellow silk. The title in yellow silk.

4   5   6

Crown jewels.

Detail of oak and laurel sprays, and stems at base.

The ground is dark blue cloth (almost black), and the whole of the embroidery is in silk. also the lace and fringe. Length of banner (without the fringe) full 42 ins. Depth at the ends 21 ins. In centre 21½ ins. and in the curves 20¼ ins. The orb of crown (approx.), and the cloth ground colour, are shown at No.8. Both sprays entirely yellow silk.

Inch scale for Nos. 2, 4, 5, 6 and 7.

Inch scale for No. 1.

on the grey drum horse as the mounted band paraded at Retford camp 1907 (Fig. 16). On this occasion the band was in undress, plain deep green frocks, chains on shoulders, green peaked caps with yellow bands and no cap badges. From the photograph[1] it can be seen that the outer sides of the banners were only about 9 ins. deep, then curving inwards for about the same measurement before connecting with the central section which was of a wide reversed bell shape, hanging below the rider's knees. The colours were likely to have been a rich dark green, gold fringe all round, embroidery, etc., of gold wire or yellow piping. The ornamentation probably consisted of the crest of Viscount Galway, within a shield, a crown above and surrounded by a wreath, the whole occupying the central bell-shaped panel, whilst interwoven letters are at left and right of crown. On the left SR (Sherwood Rangers) and probably RT on the right (believed Retford Troop).

It may be gathered from the above description that the banners were nothing like the pattern shown on Chart No. 3 and cigarette card No. 26.

[1.] Thanks are expressed to Paul North for kind loan of this photograph and to R. J. Marrion for the copy.

The South Nottinghamshire Hussars

In 1863 the dismounted band of the South Notts. Hussars was called upon on two separate occasions to perform at county functions, both events considered important enough to warrant a report and illustration in the *Illustrated London News*[1]. At this time the band in full dress was distinguished from the remainder of the Regiment, by wearing scarlet plumes in their shakos, the regimental pattern of blue cloth with black plume, the shako a kepi-like model similar to that previously worn by the regular Light Dragoons. One of the illustrations shows the band in shakos, whilst the other picture shows forage caps, the latter scarlet. In November 1865 the Hussar busby was introduced for the Regiment with a scarlet bag and scarlet and white plume, for the band an all-scarlet plume.

It is recorded that in 1858 the Regiment was presented with a pair of kettle-drum banners, but there are very few pictures showing them in use. A photograph taken in Nottingham 1887, shows a full regimental mounted parade, no drum banners in use on the drums. There is a photograph of the 1890s however, in the Regimental History[2], showing 'The Regimental Band on the march in full dress'. Here the banners are shown; the drum horse and several of the band horses are greys.

It is interesting to note that in the 1920s when the History was in course of preparation, an artist of military subjects, B. T. A. Griffiths of Newport, Mon., was sent on loan an original drum banner, together with various uniform pieces, as a guide for his colour plates. His page of notes showing the minutae of lace and design, is included here (Fig. 17). In accompanying correspondence he stresses the fact that the colour of the actual banner was a very dark blue and that the yellow silk embroidery was not a strong colour. It can be seen therefore that the Chart No. 29 shows an entirely wrong shade of blue but is otherwise quite a fair version of the original, the colouring on cigarette card No. 35 on the other hand shows near correct colouring.

Fig. 18: Q.O. Oxfordshire Hussars. Presented 1896.

This Regiment retained full dress as long as it could, i.e., up to c. 1912. There is a note that the mounted band and advance guard led the Regiment off to the annual camp, all in full dress, and that during Colonel Rolleston's period of command the band was always a mounted one. A photograph of 1907 shows the whole Regiment in mounted review order at Clifton Pastures, pill-box caps replacing Hussar busbies on this occasion, the mounted band on the right flank.

Apart from the dismounted section representing the Regiment in the Coronation Processions in London, 1911, the band and a mounted detachment took a prominent part in the celebrations at Nottingham.

1. I.L.N. 1 September 1863, Bashford Park, Nottingham, and 31 October 1863 at the ceremony when the Duke of Newcastle laid the corner-stone of the Government School of Art and Design, Nottingham.
2. *Historical Records of the South Nottinghamshire Hussars Yeomanry, 1794-1924*, by George Fellows and Engineer Commander Benson Freeman, R.N., Pub. Gale & Polden, Aldershot, 1928.

The Queen's Own Oxfordshire Hussars
Four Troops were raised in Oxfordshire in 1798, but these, together with others raised in the intervening years were not joined as a regiment until about 1818; the command of the new regiment was held by Lord Francis Churchill, 2nd son of the 4th Duke of Marlborough. Lord Francis Churchill was created Baron Churchill in 1815. The title 'Queen's Own' was granted in 1835 after Queen Adelaide, William IV's consort, had stayed in Oxford for a few days when escorts and guards were found by the Oxfordshire Yeomanry Cavalry. Queen Adelaide's cypher was later to appear on the kettle-drum banners, together with the title Queen's Own Oxfordshire Hussars, the 'Queen's Own' title the first granted to any Yeomanry Regiment. It is said that mantua purple was a colour favoured by Queen Adelaide, and adopted by the Regiment as facing colour, although described as crimson in Sleigh's 1850 *List* and in subsequent *Army Lists* until the 1890s when mantua purple appears.

An undated photograph of the mounted band[1] thought to be c. 1895 by reason of the fact that the band horses have white head-ropes and not chains (the former introduced about 1893), shows 11 musicians, a mounted kettle-drummer and the Bandmaster. The drums are uncovered, the drum horse a dark dapple grey and remainder are dark, apart from three distinctive greys.

It is recorded that in 1896 a new pair of handsome kettle-drums were presented by Surgeon Lieut.-Colonel H. P. Symonds and that a shabraque for the drum horse was given by Major L. Noble[2]. It is possible that drum banners would have been acquired about this time; a very handsome pair in mantua purple cloth, the Regimental cypher and a laurel wreath in silver, an Imperial crown in gold and a triple scroll of red cloth with the title QUEEN'S OWN — OXFORDSHIRE — HUSSARS worked in silver thread. There is a double silver lace edging with the Royal purple light between, a silver fringe all round including the top (Fig. 18). It will be noticed that Chart No. 22 is accurate, and also cigarette card No. 46 — with the exception of silver crown. The drum horse is illustrated in the *Navy & Army Illustrated* article already mentioned, the rider in

full dress, the drum banners clearly shown and the new shabraque just visible. The horse has a white out of purple throat plume and also special silver gorget-shaped plate ornamenting the head harness.

The *London Gazette* of 29 July 1896 announced that H.R.H. The Prince of Wales was appointed to the Colonelcy of the Regiment and the following year made known his intention of inspecting the Corps on 12 May. A photograph appearing in the *Illustrated London News* of 22 May 1897 shows H.R.H. leading the Regiment through St. Giles after the review, the Prince of Wales resplendent in the rich full dress as are all troops, the mounted band at the head of the parade.

The Oxfordshire Yeomanry Cavalry Regiment was one that managed to maintain its mounted band throughout King Edward's reign. There is a photograph of about 1904[3] showing that all the band had greys, the drum horse as previously described. The kettle-drummer and bandsmen have uniforms consisting of blue frocks with shoulder chains, mantua purple collar and cuffs, collar badges, blue pantaloons and blue puttees. By c. 1907-08 the same kettle-drummer, having added a few pounds weight during the intervening years, appears in our illustration Fig.19[4], and again by 1908-09[5]. On this occasion he leads the mounted band whilst on manoeuvres, the drum horse, the same grey, is equipped as for review whilst the drummer and musicians wear khaki service dress.

Whilst there is no further evidence of the band mounted, the Regiment nevertheless maintained a band for dismounted occasions under Bandmaster J. Wilson. Not only did it have a fine reputation for its musical excellence, but in uniform made a striking impression — Hussar tunics with six rows of white chest braid, mantua purple collar and cuffs, peaked caps of same colour and overalls with purple stripes. In 1909 the band could boast a strength of as many as 37 bandsmen.

1, 3, 4 & 5. At the National Army Museum.
2.   Published in the *Navy & Army Illustrated* of 10 August 1901.

The Shropshire Yeomanry Cavalry
The numerous troops raised in the county of Shropshire from 1795 were eventually amalgamated to form three regiments, later reduced to two — the North Salopian Corps and the South Salopian Regiment, both finally merged in 1872 to form the Shropshire Yeomanry Cavalry.

Whilst Regimental records make several references to the band, there are no known pictures or photographs of a mounted band, although it is certain one would have existed. In 1876 Government support ceased for the Regimental band and from then on it was maintained from the Officers' Mess Fund.

The wife of the Commanding Officer, Colonel C. G. Wingfield, presented a pair of kettle-drum banners on 8 May 1885, and these are now in the Regimental Museum at the Castle, Shrewsbury. There is a difference in size, 46 ins. and 42 ins. respectively, both 20 ins. deep, a blue ground and gold lace edging at top, a slightly wider line at the bottom with a blue portion between it and the gold fringe. The main design is a

Fig. 19: Q.O. Oxfordshire Hussars. Drum horse with 1896 banners, c. 1904.

No. 28 are quite unknown; banners of this description, *i.e.*, carrying the county arms, the loggerheads (three leopard's faces) have never been traced[1].

[1]. I am most grateful to Mr. G. Archer Parfitt, F.M.A., F.C.I.I., for his generous help with these notes.

SOMERSET

North Somerset Yeomanry

There is very little recorded about the band until the late Victorian era. A note of 1 November 1842 tells that a Mr. Donegani, formerly Troop Sergeant-Major, 4th Dragoon Guards, and late Bandmaster of 2nd Dragoon Guards, was appointed Bandmaster to the North Somerset Yeomanry. Reference to A.M.O.T. Booklet No. 2, *North Somerset Yeomanry*, describes and illustrates the complete succession of uniforms from the beginnings until 1914. Also included is a photograph of the kettle-drummer of *c.* 1889, showing to advantage the fine silver drums, without banners, one of which is illustrated on our Chart at No. 9. The drums, now held by the Somerset Military Museum Trust at Taunton, were made by Henry Potter, are silver plated with the Regimental crests of silver and the wreaths in gilt metal.

There is no conclusive evidence that drum banners were ever used, although a pair does exist and is also with the Somerset Military Museum Trust, previously at the National Army Museum. The design of these banners is quite unique, they are made of royal blue material, the scrolls at top and bottom are scarlet and piped in chain mail, which is proud of the banners; the star is of the same detail. The badge on the right is silver on a scarlet backing. It has a St. Edward's crown above a pair of laurel wreaths in the centre of which is 'VR'. The centre of the badge is fully filled in silver[1] (Fig. 21).

In 1887 Richard Simkin produced a watercolour, reproduced as a print for the Hampshire Yeomanry Cavalry; the same print has been reproduced in another state to fit the North Somerset Yeomanry, both regiments having a blue Dragoon uniform. Here the

crown over the interwoven cypher V R, oakleaf sprigs left and right, and a triple scroll below with the title SHROPSHIRE YEOMANRY CAVALRY, in gold lettering on a red ground, gold edging to scroll (Fig. 20). The pattern shown on Chart No. 5 and the cigarette card

Fig. 20: Shropshire Yeomanry. Presented 1885.

Fig. 21: North Somerset Yeomanry. Date not known, believed 1890s.

North Somerset band are shown mounted on greys, the bandsmen have red helmet plumes and the blue drum banners are edged with red lace.

1. I am grateful to Lt.-Colonel R. G. Woodhouse of the Somerset Military Museum Trust, for valued assistance and information concerning both North and West Somerset Yeomanries.

West Somerset Yeomanry

One of the first troops raised in West Somerset, the Bridgwater Troop, dates from June 1794 whilst, with other troops, a regiment was formed in 1798, the West Somerset Regiment of Yeomanry Cavalry. One of the earliest indications of a band uniform appears in a Martens' watercolour of 1846 showing two officers and a trumpeter. The author of the accompanying notes, the late L. E. Buckell states:

Fig. 22: West Somerset Yeomanry. Made in 1894.

Fig. 23: Q.O. Staffordshire Yeomanry. Band at Lulworth Cove Camp 1955.

'Attention is drawn to the trumpeter in the background of Martens' drawing. His uniform is similar to that of the private, except that an all-red plume replaces the red and white worn by the others. There is a tradition, with very little to support it, that the band and trumpeters had scarlet overalls for full dress, but as the tradition is hazy as to whether the stripes were yellow or light blue "like the French", confirmation is needed before this is accepted[1]'.

Sleigh gives strength of band in 1850 as 32.

A pair of kettle-drums, painted with the Royal Arms and with an inscription to the effect that they were presented to the West Somerset Yeomanry Cavalry by Colonel Portman in July 1854, are now with the Somerset Military Museum Trust at Taunton. Also with the Trust are a pair of drum banners made in 1894 to commemorate the centenary of the Regiment. The description of these banners is as follows: Scarlet with 1¾ ins. silver lace around edge. In centre St. Edward's crown, on left '1794' and right '1894', 'VR' beneath. The title WEST SOMERSET YEOMANRY on dark blue velvet triple scroll. At bottom the words 'Presented by Ye Faire Maids of Taunton Deane', all in silver lace (Fig. 22).

The *Somerset County Herald* for 22 September 1900 describes in detail a ceremony which took place on the preceding Monday at Vivary Park, Taunton, when yet a further pair of drum banners, and a silver bowl, were presented to the Regiment. The band under the direction of Bandmaster F. J. Moore was present, later playing selections of music in front of the Castle Hotel.

The newspaper provides a description of the banners which agrees with that shown on our Chart No. 23 and with cigarette card No. 45. 'The Mayoress then fastened the beautiful banners of scarlet cloth, heavily bordered with silver lace and fringe, to the drums of the Regiment. In the centre of the banners was shown the letters "VR" and below was the title of the Regiment. Conspicuously displayed were the dates 1800 on one

side (left) and 1900 on the other (right). At the end of each banner were the words "Presented by Ye Fair Maids of Taunton"[1]. (In a very long-winded speech made by a local dignitary he compared the 1900 'faire maids of Taunton' with earlier ladies who had presented banners to the army of the Duke of Monmouth.)

1. J.A.H.R. Vol. XXXII, page 1.

The Staffordshire Yeomanry (Queen's Own Royal Regiment)

Although the Regimental History[1] tells us that a band was formed in 1809 and that in 1818 the colour of the jackets of band and trumpeters was white with blue braid, details of band history are sparse until 1845. In May of that year 12 silver trumpets were delivered as a testimonial subscribed by local corporations for the

Fig. 24: Loyal Suffolk Hussars. Date not known, believed 1880s.

24

Regiment's service in riots in the area in 1842. (These trumpets still exist with the Regimental silver.) In 1872 a Mr. John Gladman officiated as Bandmaster for the first time and by 1881 strength of the band was 18.

It is believed that fine quality drum banners were obtained around the turn of the century and these are now preserved in the National Army Museum; their appearance suggests that they would have received little, if any, wear. Prints and photographs showing the band and these banners are rare.

The Stafford knot, with crown above, occupies the centre ground of the blue cloth banner. There is a white fringe at the top and the unusual feature of a double layer of fringes at the bottom, these consisting of alternate blocks of white (or silver) and scarlet. All four sides of the blue surface are edged with triangles of alternate red and white lace. The effect of the decorations give these banners a most attractive appearance, and show us that Chart No. 4 and cigarette card No. 27 are incorrect in various ways.

Fig. 23 is a photograph of the Q.O.R.R. Yeomanry band at Lulworth Cove in 1955. The Bandmaster and all bandsmen wear blue patrol uniforms with scarlet collars and it will be noted that almost all are old soldiers with Second World War medals[2].

1. *The Records of the Queen's Own Royal Regiment of Staffordshire Yeomanry* by P. C. G. Webster. Pub. 1870.
2. I am grateful for the assistance with these notes kindly given by Christopher Coogan, and also to Mr. M. Holland for producing the photograph; both are members of the West Midlands M.H.S. Branch.

The Loyal Suffolk Hussars

It is not the purpose of these notes to enter into the argument about the date when this Regiment was raised, but as it has a bearing on the drum banners of later years, then a word here may be appropriate. The official date of acceptance and commission is given as May 1794[1] but the Regiment has always maintained that it should be 1793, this date being given in an article by a member of the corps using the nom de plume 'Scribbler'. Here it is stated: 'the regiment was formed in 1793, and was consequently one of the first yeomanry regiments in existence.' Another statement from the same source spans 100 years and records that: The Loyal Suffolk Hussars was the regiment selected to have conferred upon it the honour of being used as a means of associating the Duke of York with the cavalry, and in July 1892, His Royal Highness was appointed hon. colonel, two years later the prefix "Duke of York's Own" being granted.

So with a Royal Colonel, an up to strength quota of enthusiastic men from Suffolk, Norfolk, Cambridgeshire and Essex, and a glorious green and gold uniform (a reminder of the ten years 1868-1878 when the Regiment had a green Dragoon uniform) who could blame 'Scribbler' for his egotistical opinion. The concluding paragraph from the magazine brings one to the band: 'The band of the Loyal Suffolk Hussars must not be forgotten, as few yeomanry regiments possess its equal, none better; this being due to the great interest taken in its efficiency by the Bandmaster, Quartermaster W. H. Heal, late 20th Hussars.'

Fig. 25: Loyal Suffolk Hussars. Mounted band and kettle drummer, late 1890s.

Mr. Heal came to the Regiment in 1894 having reached the rank of Sergeant-Major, 20th Hussars, in May 1891, and was eventually promoted Lieutenant in May 1903. Captain J. Whitaker, also 20th Hussars, was the Adjutant at this period and the permanent staff was drawn from the 18th Hussars and 9th Lancers. Thus the Regiment was fortunate to have contacts with regular cavalry from Colchester and Norwich.

A former officer of the Regiment with pre-1914 service relates how difficult it was for a Yeomanry corps to train a drum horse, a task of many months if done properly, and so it was often easier to borrow a drum horse, and often the drummer, from the regulars, who often had a spare[2]. Between the 1880s, and just after 1900 or thereabouts when the band ceased to parade mounted, one can account for at least three horses — a splendid piebald, a chestnut and an all-white or cream horse[3] (Fig. 25).

Drum banners are thought to date from the 1880s and were carefully noted and sketched, together with uniforms and contents from many photograph albums, then the property of 358 (Suffolk Yeomanry) R.A. (T.A.), at Bury St. Edmunds, in 1954. The banners were of deep blue-green silk, edged ¼ inch gold braid and gold bullions. Crown gold with silver pearls and crimson velvet inside hoops, garter red velvet, gold edge and letters. Castle silver on green centre, 1793 below. Red velvet triple scroll below with the title LOYAL SUFFOLK HUSSARS in gold thread (Fig. 24). The versions on Chart No. 25 and cigarette card No. 42 show numerous errors. A special shabraque was designed for use on the drum horse, green with gold double edging, a wreath and castle badge worked on the hind sections.

1. The Correct Precedence Table compiled by Engineer Commander Benson Freeman, R.N., can be found published in the 1928 *Regimental History of the South Notts Hussars*.
2. From correspondence in this writer's possession, also some pages of notes made by the late L. E. Buckell during his 1954 visit.
3. The piebald horse and drummer, both from a cavalry regiment, but with the kettle-drummer wearing Suffolk Hussars' uniform, appeared as a photographic illustration in *The Regiment*, 3 September 1898. The chestnut drum horse may have belonged to the Regiment and is featured in our illustration.

The artist James Prinsep Beadle painted the scene when the mounted Regiment paraded in review order before H.R.H. The Duke of York at Bury St. Edmunds on 27 May 1893. The mounted band was in evidence, Prinsep showing the piebald drum horse, although a photograph shows the chestnut, but the latter occasion may have been for a full dress rehearsal.

Fig. 27: Royal Wiltshire Yeomanry. Kettle-drummer in camp 1901. Note khaki helmet with van dyke puggri for band.

Westmorland and Cumberland Yeomanry

One of our pictures[1] (Fig. 26) shows the scene in the market square of a Lake District town, probably Penrith in 1887. The townsfolk have turned out on a less than pleasant day to join in the local celebrations for Queen Victoria's Golden Jubilee — the weather obviously has not dampened their spirits. A police inspector in mounted full dress and several stalwart constables were sufficient to keep things orderly, and the local fire brigade, wearing brass helmets, were standing by in a side street. A small band from the Border Regiment, in full dress scarlet, was on parade, and the local Yeomanry band drawn up on the right appeared in all its finery. The Bandmaster on a splendid cream horse, together with the kettle-drummer, are in the foreground, the nearside view of the latter shows the uniform, drum banner and horse furniture to advantage. The sheepskin bridle cover has a scalloped edge, the shabraque is decorated on the hind section with the same design as that of the banner, the interwoven letters WCYC with a crown above and sprays below. The drum banner is thought to be scarlet with silver or white edging and has a fringe at the bottom, also the most unusual feature of teeth, or points of white cloth as part of the edging both top and bottom.

No. 4 in the A.M.O.T. Yeomanry series devotes a chapter to the band and describes the dress in detail whilst the drum horse and drummer are reproduced as a cover painting in full colour. Also shown are two photographs of the mounted kettle-drummer of *c.* 1912 and *c.* 1914, the first in full dress with pill-box cap, the second in khaki service dress. Chart No. 11 shows gilt drum casing but the drums illustrated in Booklet No. 4 have stencilled white semi-circular panels carrying titles, etc. It is possible that these drums in the 1912 and 1914 pictures were kept for drills or field use, and the fact that the Regiment could still turn out a properly equipped drum horse up to 1914 suggests that a mounted band may also have been a possibility.

1. This has been trimmed so that the principal feature of the drum horse are prominent.

Fig. 26: Westmorland and Cumberland Yeomanry. Mounted band and kettle-drummer, believed photographed at Penrith, possibly 1887.

The Royal Wiltshire Yeomanry (Prince of Wales's Own Royal Regiment)

In January 1831 the Wiltshire Yeomanry Cavalry became the first Yeomanry regiment to receive the honorary and distinctive title of 'Royal', thus styled the Royal Wiltshire Regiment of Yeomanry Cavalry, a mark of appreciation from His Majesty for services rendered during local serious disturbances[1]. A further honour was to follow in April 1863 when the title 'Prince of Wales's Own' was conferred on the Regiment, thus being the first regiment of Yeomanry Cavalry that had had the honour of attending the Prince of Wales as escort on the occasion of his visit to Savernake on 10 February 1863.

It is possible that, although the Regiment had long possessed a band, new drum banners may have been acquired about this time. A photograph taken at Devizes in 1883 shows the mounted band in full Hussar dress, with possibly as many as 20 mounted musicians. The drum horse is of mixed colour, whilst amongst the remainder of band horses there are at least four greys.

The actual drum banners differ in several particulars from those shown on the Chart, illustration No. 1, and on the 1924 cigarette card No. 24; the colour of cloth is deep crimson, lace edging and fringe is gold, not silver as shown. With the exception of the Prince of Wales's feathers which are white, all other lace is gold. The Crest of England, a golden crested lion standing on an Imperial crown (without protruding on to the border edging as shown) rests on the garter which carries the motto 'HONI SOIT QUI MAL Y PENSE' in gold embroidered lettering on a blue velvet ground. The Regimental title, 'WILTSHIRE' and 'YEOMANRY' appear on separate scrolls left and right, again with gold print on blue background at the foot of the banner. The actual drums carried the Prince of Wales's feather plume in raised silver and embossed on the drum casings.

In spite of the beautiful rich quality of the drum banners they apparently accompanied the band to camp each year (Fig. 27) borne out by photographs taken during the late 1890s and early 1900s.

The uniform of the kettle-drummer at this time consisted of blue tunic and pantaloons but the headdress a khaki helmet, the band helmets distinguished by a vandyke patterned puggri; the Prince of Wales's metal badge worn on the puggri at front, on collars and as N.C.O.s' arm-badge.

It is believed that the present Regiment, now a Squadron of the Royal Regiment of Yeomanry, still possesses the old Squadron Standards and the drum banners[2] (Fig. 28).

[1] *The Annals of the Yeomanry Cavalry of Wiltshire.* By Henry Graham, pub. 1886
[2] Certainly up to the 1950s, see photograph in *Soldier* magazine, February 1951.

YORKSHIRE

The Queen's Own Yorkshire Yeomanry, the modern Regiment dating from 1956, was a composite from the three old county regiments of 1914 and beyond, *i.e.*, the Yorkshire Hussars, the Yorkshire Dragoons and the East Riding of Yorkshire Yeomanry. The Hussars had a continuous existence from 1794; the Yorkshire Dragoons succeeded the 1st West Yorkshire Yeomanry Cavalry in 1897; finally the East Riding Regiment — although originated in the 1790s — was one of the modern regiments raised after the South African War in April 1902.

A.M.O.T. have published booklets on the Yorkshire Hussars and the Dragoons, Nos. 3 and 7 respectively, where uniforms and details of the bands are very well documented. It is probably true to say that the reputations of the bands of both Regiments were second to none in the Yeomanry, with possible exception of the Northumberland Hussars. Both are known to have had mounted bands throughout their histories and yet, although almost certainly the most photographed in the country, including the regular cavalry, not a single print is known showing drum banners in use nor the whereabouts of the actual banners. So we must accept the representations on the Chart as it is most likely that the artist was able to obtain data during his researches.

The Yorkshire Hussars

In 1852 the artist Michael Angelo Hayes, working on a commission from the Regiment, painted an album of watercolour sketches showing the uniforms *From the Embodiment of their Foundation to the Present Time — 1852*. Included in this beautiful series, Plate No. 24 shows the kettle-drummer of 1848, the drummer in the Light Dragoon uniform of the day with pale blue shako and pelisse, the drums without banners.

The representation of the drum banner, Chart No. 2 and cigarette card No. 25, show a black banner but there is reason to believe that it was in fact a very dark shade of scarlet.

Fig. 28: Royal Wiltshire Yeomanry. The drum banners as shown in Fig. 27, photographed after 1920 at R.H.Q.

In later years both the Hussars and Dragoons would parade on Military Sunday, the Hussars marching on foot through York in dismounted review order, a great occasion for the townsfolk and for photographers in particular.

The Yorkshire Dragoons

Sleigh's List of 1850 gives the strength of the band of the 1st West Yorkshire Yeomanry Cavalry as 24. Certainly from this date onwards the history of the Regiment and the succeeding Dragoons is particularly well documented. There is an excellent chapter on the band in Booklet No. 7 where a photograph of the mounted band has been published. The date given is *c.* 1899 and is believed to be the only picture of this mounted band. The bandsmen are in drill order, the drums have white semi-circular panels with titles, etc., on the shells.

Chart No. 8 and cigarette card No. 31 show the white rose and title Queen's Own, the latter conferred in 1897.

The distinguished Bandmaster of this Regiment from 1873 was Mr. Samuel Suckley, who from 1872 until 1898 had the unique distinction of holding the position of Field (or Commanding Officer's) Trumpeter. In 1892 he was commissioned 2nd Lieutenant. This is the only known occasion of a C.O.'s Trumpeter becoming a commissioned officer. He retired in 1914[1]. His son Samuel Cramer Suckley was Bandmaster of the Yorkshire Hussars, both regimental bands earning brilliant country-wide reputations.

[1.] *Yorkshire Contemporary Bibliographies.* Also the account by R. J. Smith in Booklet No. 7.

YEOMANRY DRUM BANNERS NOT ON THE GALE & POLDEN SHEET
The Royal Bucks Hussars

Reference to a band, almost certainly mounted, can be found in Regimental records for 1831 and again in 1845. Half a century later we find that:

'In the summer of 1897 a great honour was conferred on the Royal Bucks Hussars. On Monday 21st June, a strong squadron, some 150 strong, of the regiment, accompanied by the band, assembled at Beaconsfield, consisting of men specially picked, for escort duty in welcoming back H.M. Queen Victoria to her Castle at Windsor, after the Diamond Jubilee celebration in London. At twelve o'clock next day the regiment was marshalled in the High Street, from whence it started, headed by the band, for the Household Cavalry Barracks at Windsor to join the Royal Horse Guards, with which regiment it was to act in forming the field officer's escort of Her Majesty from Slough to Windsor. After the reception at Slough, the squadron escorted the Queen to Windsor, and on arrival at the Castle, Colonel Lord Chesham was presented to Her Majesty and by her special command the whole of the troopers filed past her carriage as it stood in the Quadrangle.'

A photograph of the squadron taken at Beaconsfield shows the mounted band in review order, positioned on the left flank, and headed by a fine skewbald drum horse. The kettle-drums are without covers.

Banners were obtained during King Edward's reign, no doubt after the award of the battle honour 'South Africa 1900-1901', and the approval by the Army Council of a new badge for the Regiment in lieu of the old Maltese Cross. This badge, a silver cygnet and motto appears on the new deep green banners (a shade which is almost blue) above the title Royal Bucks Hussars and the 'South Africa' battle honour scroll[1] (Fig. 30). The banners were much in use at the Coronation celebrations of 1911 and a photograph appears in a county military history[2] showing a detachment under Colonel The Hon. Harry Lawson, T.D., parading in Beaconsfield on 1 July 1911, previous to escorting H.M. King George V from Slough to Windsor on his first visit there after his coronation. A detail from this picture is reproduced here (Fig. 29). It will be seen that the drum horse is now a grey with white throat plume, and the remainder of band horses are dark, all bandsmen wear review order uniform. The Bandmaster, Mr. Padfield, who held the appointment from 1902-1914, can be seen beside the kettle-drummer.

Other photographs of the period between 1900 and 1914 show that the band invariably accompanied the Regiment to camp and almost always appeared in full dress.

Fig. 29: Royal Bucks Hussars. Coronation detachment and band. Parade at Beaconsfield 1st July 1911.

1. Now at the National Army Museum, photo reproduced by kind permission.
2. *The Citizen Soldiers of Buckinghamshire, 1795-1926* by Major-General J. C. Swann, C.B., D.L. Pub. by the Buckinghamshire T.A. Association 1930.

The East Devon Volunteer Cavalry 1794-1838

In 1803 five Troops of Yeomanry Cavalry, six Companies of Infantry and two Artillery Companies were joined together under the name of the East Devon Legion. The Legion as such was a short-lived body disbanding in 1808, but the Yeomanry Cavalry section continued on as late as 1838. In 1827 there is a reference to a band of the Legion Cavalry although an Order of 28 January 1828 announced the disbandment of the East Devon Legion Yeomanry Cavalry, three Troops at Hemyock, Honiton and Churchstanton surviving until 1838.

A pair of drum banners passed through an auction house during 1956, the catalogue description: 'Pair of drum banners of the East Devon Volunteer Cavalry, 26 ins. x 20 ins., pale yellow with watermarks of a floral pattern, Cypher of William IV, in glazed wooden frames, 36 ins. x 24 ins., Very fine' (Fig. 31). Although these may be thought small for drum banners and the cords and tassels attached might suggest trumpet banners, in any event they must be considered valuable evidence of the 1830-37 period.

ESSEX

The West Essex Yeomanry Cavalry

Amongst the most spectacular kettle-drummers of the British Army of the 1840s was the negro musician, formerly Coldstream Guards, of the West Essex Yeomanry. A colour print by J. Harris after H. Martens, published as No. 7 in Fore's Yeomanry Costumes of 1846[1] shows an officer of the Regiment in mounted review order, the mounted band and troops in the

Fig. 31: East Devon Volunteer Cavalry. 1830 37.

background. The drummer rides a white horse, the drums are of blue-grey-silver metal, the drummer's uniform is quite magnificent: High white turban, tall golden coloured upright plume, scarlet plastron on blue coatee, gilt shoulder scales and crimson pants.

The mounted band and kettle-drummer is conspicuous in an illustration showing an inspection of the West Essex Yeomanry Cavalry on Wanstead Flats in 1853[2].

1. Reproduced in colour in *The Essex Yeomanry*, Vol. 3 by J. W. Burrows. Pub. J. W. Burrows *c.* 1925.
2. *Illustrated London News* of 8 June 1853.

The Essex Yeomanry

In May 1902 drum banners had been presented and used for decorative purposes at concerts, etc., as the new Regiment of November 1901 did not have a mounted

Fig. 30: Royal Bucks Hussars. Date not known but certainly during Edwardian years.

band. These banners were of the same colour as the full dress uniform, green, with Regimental crest in gold embroidery in centre, a crown with garter carrying the Regimental motto 'Audacter et Sincere', encompassing the three Seaxes, the County Arms, on a red ground; the title ESSEX IMPERIAL YEOMANRY on a triple scroll below, gold fringe at the foot of the banner.

The kettle-drums on their stands, with these banners as covers, were mounted by a table for a presentation ceremony at Orsett camp in 1911. A photograph shows the Commanding Officer presenting the Horsemanship Cup on this occasion. In addition there were post-war photographs, firstly of a group of officers, W.O.s and N.C.O.s of the 104th (Essex Yeomanry) Brigade, R.F.A., at camp in 1922 with drums and banners similarly displayed[1]. Finally a photograph taken at Tilshead camp in 1936 shows the entire band of 20 bandsmen and Bandmaster, in green full dress with scarlet plumes, the banners over the drums on their stands.

[1.] Photograph reproduced in Burrows, Vol. 3.

The Fife Light Horse
The Regimental History[1] informs us that: 'Some days after a review of the Fife Volunteers (Mounted and Rifles), in July 1872 at Dumbarnie Links, Colonel Thompson received the following letter from Admiral Bethune: "Balfour, Markinch. A lady here on a visit, much charmed by the gallant bearing of the Light Horse has volunteered to work banners for the kettle-drums, and if you will send me the pattern and devices, I will hand them to her. Signed: Charles D. O. Bethune". In January 1873 the banners arrived. They were very valuable and beautiful works of art, the Thane of Fife being embroidered in silk in the proper Heraldic colours.'

The banners are described as scarlet material with silver lace and blue edging. Horse and rider in buff, scroll silver lace (Fig. 32).

'Some years after the drummer packed them into a portmanteau with his drum sticks and a new tunic. By some accident the portmanteau was left in the railway carriage and never seen again although diligent enquiry was made at every railway and police station.'

[1.] *The History of the Fife Light Horse* by Colonel Anstruther Thompson. Pub. W. Blackwood, 1892.

The Royal Gloucestershire Hussars
The Regiment used to have (and probably still does) a pair of drum banners kept in its Club at Gloucester; these banners were presumably in use up to 1889 when new ones were presented. There is a photograph taken at Cheltenham in May 1882 showing the Regiment on parade in mounted review order, band and drums with these banners on the right. A photograph of the drum horse with the same banners, mounted drummer in review order, is in this writer's collection but it is a very faint picture and unfortunately not suitable for reproduction, but see colour illustration on front cover. These banners were, even at that time, very old, having been presented during the reign of William IV. The size was 32 ins. x 24 ins., described as of red plush material, with a crown embroidered in full colours in the upper central position with the numerals IV below and 'W' to the left and 'R' to the right, the letters 'G Y C' below the IV, the lettering described as in dark and bright gold thread[1]. There was a fringe at the bottom (Fig. 33).

New banners were presented by the wives of the officers in 1889, described in the Regimental History[2] as richly embroidered. Apparently there are no photographs known of these new banners.

[1.] From detail supplied to the writer by Mr. Charles Lovell, Secretary of the Old Comrades Association (1956), and one time Squadron Sergeant-Major in the Regiment.
[2.] *The Yeoman Cavalry of Gloucester and Monmouth.* By W. H. Wyndham Quinn, M.P. Pub. Cheltenham 1898.

The Norfolk Yeomanry
Silver kettle-drums and drum banners were presented in 1905 although the band did not perform mounted more than once or twice. The banners, in the Regimental collection at Swaffham, are dark blue with yellow edging and tassels. The cypher, Edward VII, is in gold on a light grey ground[1].

[1.] Photograph of the banner and short chapter on the band in Booklet No. 12 in the A.M.O.T. Yeomanry series.

Royal East Kent Mounted Rifles
Little is known about any band during the early period of regimental history although a clue can be gathered from a tailor's book of 1868 describing a band music-

Fig. 32: Fife and Forfar Yeomanry. Presented 1873.

Fig. 33: Royal Gloucestershire Hussars. 1830-37.

pouch. At that time the Regiment had just changed from Kentish grey to a rifle green, and this is the uniform shown in wear by a smart dismounted band at camp in 1902[1].

There was an earlier band of course and probably an attempt was made to mount it, as described in light-hearted vein in later years by the grandson of a former Commanding Officer[2]. In 1970 Lord Guilford told a gathering of Old Comrades how his grandfather paid for a band out of his own pocket and even attempted to conduct it himself. He also related how, when this band went on parade, it had not rehearsed with horses and — 'the band went one way, the horses the other and the troops another, but the band played manfully on'.

In 1907 when the Regiment was at annual camp at Folkestone there was a mounted drill when copper drums were paraded without banners. There was no drum horse furniture and the drummer was attired as the remainder, *i.e.*, khaki cap with bronze badge, khaki

frock with scarlet collar and cuffs, steel shoulder chains and finally khaki pants and putties.

As befitting a rifle regiment, the main set of kettle-drums were painted in sombre tones, dark shells with the Royal Arms in full colours and title scrolls above and below. One photograph of *c.* 1908, taken outside a H.Q. building, shows an orchestra of 25 men (Fig. 34). All wear the rifle green 'walking-out' dress, *i.e.*, a peaked cap of green body, scarlet top and black mohair cap band, bronze badge; full dress rifle tunic with black chest braid, scarlet collar and cuffs; bandsmen have rifle aiguillettes with two brass tags, worn from left shoulder; nether-wear — overalls, half wellingtons and spurs. The Bandmaster with frock-coat and in contrast to the remainder, bright cap and collar badges and buttons. It is interesting to note that on a group photograph of the band taken at camp prior to 1914, the same Bandmaster has heavy plaited aiguillettes added to his dress; band personnel as previously described, but on this occasion could boast a full strength of about 45 musicians.

The Royal East Kent Yeomanry had the additional titles of (The Duke of Connaught's Own) (Mounted Rifles), Field Marshal H.R.H. Arthur, Duke of Connaught, being the Regiment's Honorary Colonel from 1896.

1. *Navy and Army Illustrated* of 19 July 1902.
2. The Earl of Guilford, reported in a Kent local newspaper 15 October 1970.

The Lanarkshire Yeomanry

Although a regiment with a continuous history from *c.* 1819, little evidence is available about a band, but it undoubtedly had one. A photograph[1] of *c.* 1887 shows a Squadron parade in the High Street, Lanark, the mounted band parading on the left and the mounted kettle-drummer, on a white horse, can be seen at the rear of the band, but there are no drum banners in evidence. There is also a note that in 1899 the Regimental band

Fig. 34: Royal East Kent Mtd. Rifles, *c.* 1908. Note elaborate title scrolls and crests on shells. Drums mounted on stands.

played outside the Clydesdale Hotel, Lanark Racecourse, where the Regiment was drilled, and that the programme was finished with the old hymn tune 'St. Petersburg'.

After a 40-year period it is interesting to note that new silver kettle-drums were presented to the Regiment by the Colonel, Sir John T. Usher, at Scroggs Camp, Lockerbie, and were received by the Rt. Hon. The Earl of Home, K.T., T.D., Hon. Colonel of the Regiment[2].

[1.] Photograph in A.M.O.T.
[2.] Photograph of the event published in the *Weekly Scotsman* of 29 July 1938.

London and Westminster Light Horse

Mentioned in the Introduction, accompanied by the illustration Fig. 1, is the photograph of the earliest known drum banner of Volunteer Cavalry, that of the London and Westminster Light Horse Volunteers. The banner was at one time part of the collection housed at the Royal United Services Institution Museum in Whitehall, now preserved at the National Army Museum. Writing in 1922 in the *Cavalry Journal*, Edward Fraser supplied some useful information on the banners of this Regiment and a description of the one we are able to illustrate:

'This Regiment had three pairs of drum banners, the City of London gave the First Troop its drum banners, which were crimson; King George III gave the Second Troop a pair of blue banners, and City were once again the donors of the banners to the Third Troop, which were also blue. Each of these banners, vertically divided, bears in its right half the Arms of the City of London, the white shield bearing a red St. George's Cross and the red dagger in the upper left hand quarter; on the left half are the Arms of the City of Westminster, the gold portcullis on blue on the lower two-thirds of the shield, and on the upper third, also on a blue ground, Edward the Confessor's gold cross with the four golden martlets (heraldic legless swallows), flanked by two double red and white roses. Above the Coat of Arms shield are the words "London and Westminster", and below the motto "Forward", and under the motto "Light Horse Volunteers". The ground colour of these drum banners is blue and the shield, being surmounted with a wreath of roses and thistles, proves them to be older than the Union with Ireland in 1801, when shamrocks were added to all similar wreaths on drum banners.'

There is a known painting by Wheatley of an officer of the London and Westminster — Henry Phillip Hope, dated *c.* 1811. This officer is shown holding his charger and standing outside a tent. On the ground at the tent opening are the kettle-drums and a single drumstick,

Fig. 35: Drum banner of Warwickshire Yeomanry Cavalry, early Victorian; *by courtesy of Warwickshire Yeomanry Museum.*

whilst just visible, seated inside the tent, is the negro kettle-drummer.

The Isle of Wight

For a period of nearly 30 years from 1798, various small Troops of Yeomanry existed on the Isle of Wight, the main body raised at Newport about 1818 and known as The Vectis Light Dragoons. This unit at one time reached Squadron strength mustering 113 members in two Troops, and also possessed a band. The Vectis Light Dragoons were disbanded about 1825 and then no Yeomanry existed on the Island until 1888, when a Troop was raised at Ryde for the Hampshire Carabiniers.

During its short existence the Vectis Yeomanry Band received several favourable press reports, one such describing a five-day exercise at Newport 'the good appearance of the men, the fineness of the weather and the music of their excellent band have enlivened the town'.

A kettle-drum is preserved at the Castle Museum in Newport. It is in fine condition, is painted in bright colours, the shell of deep yellow, a band of alternate yellow, red and blue stripes at the top, the motto 'Nemo Me Impune Lacesset' in gold lettering on a blue band with a coronet and star within.

2nd West Yorkshire Yeomanry Cavalry

Raised in 1798, there were three short periods of service before a disbandment in 1820 — re-raised in 1843 and finally disbanded in 1894. During these last years the Regiment had a mounted band.

There were four pages of pictures in the *Illustrated London News* of 15 August 1863 when the Regiment under Colonel Henry Edwards, M.P., escorted the royal carriage during the visit to Halifax of H.R.H. The Prince of Wales. The mounted band is shown in two of the illustrations playing outside the town hall.

Notes on Yeomanry Regimental Bands Both Mounted and Dismounted

Bedfordshire: Dismounted band. Post-1902.

Denbighshire: Band revived 1853. Disbanded 1902.

Glamorgan: Dismounted band. Post-1902.

Hertfordshire: Believed mounted band up to *c.* 1902. Dismounted from that date.

Lanarkshire: Mounted band pre-1901/2. Dismounted from that date.

Leicestershire: Mounted band recorded during 1890s.

Lincolnshire: Dismounted band. Post-1902.

Westminster Dragoons: Mounted band known in 1902.

Northamptonshire: Dismounted band. Post-1902.

Pembroke. The Castlemartin Yeomanry: A pair of well preserved kettle-drums were sold by auction in 1977,